## ALSO BY BRUCE M. METZGER

The Saturday and Sunday Lessons from Luke in the Greek Gospel Lectionary

A Guide to the Preparation of a Thesis

Index of Articles on the New Testament and the Early Church published in Festschriften

Annotated Bibliography of the Textual Criticism of the New Testament

The Text, Canon, and Principal Versions of the Bible (with E. E. Flack)

An Introduction to the Apocrypha

Index to Periodical Literature on the Apostle Paul

Lists of Words Occurring Frequently in the Coptic New Testament

The Oxford Concise Concordance to the Revised Standard Version of the Holy Bible (with Isobel M. Metzger)

Chapters in the History of New Testament Textual Criticism

The Text of the New Testament, its Transmission, Corruption, and Restoration (also in German, Japanese, and Mandarin)

Index to Periodical Literature on Christ and the Gospels

The New Testament, its Background, Growth, and Content

Historical and Literary Studies: Pagan, Jewish, and Christian

A Textual Commentary on the Greek New Testament

The Early Versions of the New Testament, their Origin, Transmission, and Limitations

New Testament Studies, Philological, Versional, and Patristic

Manuscripts of the Greek Bible, an Introduction to Greek ·Palaeography

*Editor of:*

New Testament Tools and Studies ( 10 vols.)

Twentieth Century Encyclopedia of Religious Knowledge (New Testament Editor)

The Oxford Annotated Bible (with Herbert G. May)

The Oxford Annotated Apocrypha

The United Bible Societies' Edition of the Greek New Testament (with K. Aland, M. Black, C. M. Martini, and A. Wikgren)

The Reader's Digest Condensed Bible

# LEXICAL AIDS FOR STUDENTS OF NEW TESTAMENT GREEK

BRUCE M. METZGER

*George L. Collord Professor of*
*New Testament Language and Literature*
*Princeton Theological Seminary*

NEW EDITION

PUBLISHED BY THE AUTHOR

Distributed by the Theological Book Agency
CN 821
Princeton, New Jersey

1983

οὐ πόλλ' ἀλλὰ πολύ   'not quantity but quality'

(*literally*, 'not many things but much')


μελέτη τὸ πᾶν   'practice makes perfect'

(*literally*, 'practice [is] everything')

# PREFACE

ACCORDING to the psychologist, one learns by associating the new with the old, the strange with the familiar. In studying a foreign language, therefore, the beginner will do well to observe whatever similarities may exist between his own and the other language.

Part I of the following *Lexical Aids* makes use of this principle of associative learning by supplying, after the English definitions of Greek words, such English derivatives as may be of assistance in remembering the meaning of the Greek vocabulary. The Greek words in the list, furthermore, have been selected and arranged in accord with their frequency of occurrence in the New Testament.

Part II makes a different application of the same psychological principle. Here are exhibited the family relationships among words of frequent and less frequent occurrence. After a student has become acquainted with a minimum working vocabulary of words that occur many times in the New Testament he can make more rapid progress in acquiring a larger vocabulary by learning such additional words as resemble in general meaning and form those which he already knows.

What proportion of attention should be devoted to Part I ('Words Classified According to Their Frequency') before beginning to employ at the same time Part II ('Words Classified According to Their Root') can be determined on the basis of economy of time and effort. A judicious and faithful use of both Parts will speed the day when the beginner can read the Greek Testament with pleasure and profit.

*October 1, 1946*

# PREFACE TO THE ENLARGED EDITION

AT the time of the sixth printing of this little book, it is appropriate to accede to the requests of some who have used it in the classroom that future printings include a list of the principal parts of verbs which occur most frequently in the New Testament. Accordingly, Appendix IV has been added to this enlarged edition. Furthermore, in order to provide assistance in another area of New Testament lexicography, a list is given in Appendix V of all the nouns of the second declension that end in -ος and are feminine in gender.

Perhaps it may be confessed here that the Greek colophon that stands on the last page is doubly appropriate—no less for the compiler than for the user of this booklet. This couplet, with which many a weary scribe in the Byzantine period brought his manuscript to a close, may be rendered, 'As travelers rejoice to see their native land, so also is the end of a book to those who labor!'

*December 16, 1954*

# PREFACE TO THE NEW EDITION

THIS new edition differs from the previous ones more in form than in content. The two earlier editions, which went through fourteen printings totalling 60,000 copies, were reproduced from the typescript copy prepared by the author; the present edition has been photo-lithoprinted from type set by the skilled craftsmen of the University Press at Oxford.

At the same time, the adoption of a new format has made it possible to incorporate a number of modifications in the contents. Minor adjustments have been made in several of the definitions, and the number of English derivatives has been increased. The bibliography of Greek lexicons (see pp. 5-6) has been revised in the light of recent publications. In response to requests made by several teachers, the present edition has been supplied with an alphabetical index of the Greek words that are included in the frequency word lists.

BRUCE M. METZGER

*February 9, 1969*

# CONTENTS

PART I

# WORDS CLASSIFIED ACCORDING TO THEIR FREQUENCY

ACCORDING to statistics collected by Robert Morgenthaler,[1] the Greek New Testament makes use of 5,436 different Greek words. More than one half of these (namely, 3,246 words) occur only once, twice, or thrice in the entire New Testament. Of the remainder, about eleven hundred occur ten or more times. All of these, with the exception of proper names,[2] are included in the following word lists (comprising a total of 1,067 words), and are arranged in descending order of their frequency.

The usefulness of such lists is obvious. By consulting them the beginner will not, so to speak, waste his time memorizing words that occur only rarely in the New Testament. He can be assured that when he has learned, say, the first 513 words in the lists he then knows *all* of the words (other than the proper names) that occur at least 25 times in the New Testament.

The beginner of any foreign language always finds it easier to acquire a working knowledge of the vocabulary if he is shown parallels between it and his own language. Although several grammars for beginners of Classical Greek are provided with such mnemonic aids (as, for example, the grammars by H. L. Crosby and J. N. Schaeffer, and by A. S. Way), grammarians of New Testament Greek have been slow in adopting this pedagogically sound procedure. As a start in this direction there have been added to the following frequency word lists such English derivatives as seemed likely to prove helpful to the student

[1] *Statistik des neutestamentlichen Wortschatzes* (Zurich, 1958). The statistics are based on the 21st edition of the Nestle Greek New Testament. According to Morgenthaler (p. 26), the total number of words in the entire Greek New Testament is 137,490 words. Every seventh word is a definite article, every fifteenth word an 'and,' and every twenty-fifth word an αὐτός. The ten most frequently used words comprise about 45,000 of the total 137,328 words, and the approximately 170 words that occur more than one hundred times each comprise about 100,000 words of the total text (that is, about five-sevenths of the New Testament).

[2] As a rule the proper names in the Greek New Testament so closely resemble the corresponding names in English as to occasion very little difficulty of recognition. A table of equivalent letters is given below on p. 3.

of New Testament Greek. It need scarcely be mentioned that not every Greek word has an English derivative. Nevertheless, a surprisingly large proportion of the following words can be supplied with more or less well-known English derivatives.[1] The derivative, which is italicized and enclosed within parentheses, is not to be confused with the definition of the Greek word. The definition is to be memorized; the derivative is intended to be of assistance in remembering the definition. Although many other examples of English derivations from these Greek words might have been cited, those which are given were chosen with an eye to the probable interests of the type of student who will make use of this booklet. That is, whenever it was possible to do so, derivatives were provided that involve theological, ecclesiastical, or patristic terminology.

In some instances the derivative is not direct but is from a closely related word in Greek. In these cases the English word is introduced by the abbreviation 'cf.' ( = 'compare'). Thus, for example, the definition of the noun διδάσκαλος is followed by '(cf. *didactic*),' for, although no noun in English is a direct derivative of διδάσκαλος, the adjective *didactic*, being derived from a closely related Greek word (διδακτικός), will serve as a mnemonic aid in remembering the meaning of διδάσκαλος. In a few instances, when not even this sort of indirect derivative is available in English, a cognate word is cited. Thus, after the definition of πατήρ one finds '(akin to *paternal*),' for *paternal* closely resembles πατήρ because the English word is derived from the Latin *pater*, which in turn is a cognate of the Greek word.[2]

Attention may be called to the occasional use of a word or phrase enclosed within parentheses in conjunction with the definition of a Greek word. Thus, ἀποστέλλω is defined '*I send* (with a commission)'. The words within parentheses will not be confused with the English derivative, for the latter is in every case printed in italics. Again, it will be observed that a semi-colon is used (1) to separate quite diverse English definitions of the same Greek word, and (2) to separate two or more English derivatives from one another.

The following table of equivalent letters and diphthongs will be of assistance in learning to become aware of many English derivatives

---

[1] To be exact, 467 of the 1066 words that occur ten times or more are provided with English derivatives. This is about 45 per cent.

[2] For further information regarding cognate words, see Appendix I.

other than those which are cited by way of example. The Greek letters whose transliteration is immediately obvious are not included.

CONSONANTS

| Greek | English | Examples |
|-------|---------|----------|
| γγ | ng | εὐαγγέλιον, evangel |
| ζ | z | ζωή, Zoe |
| κ | c (sometimes k)[1] | ἐκκλησία, ecclesiastic<br>κινέω, kinetic<br>εἰκών, icon (also ikon) |
| ξ | x | ξύλον, xylophone |
| φ | ph | φωνή, -phone |
| χ | ch | εὐχαριστία, Eucharist |
| ψ | ps | ψεύδομαι, pseudo- |

VOWELS AND DIPHTHONGS

| Greek | English | Examples |
|-------|---------|----------|
| η | e | ζωή, Zoe |
| (initial) ι (followed by a vowel) | j | ἰῶτα, jot<br>'Ιησοῦς, Jesus |
| υ | y | ψυχή, psyche |
| αι | e (or ae) | αἷμα, hemoglobin (or haemo-) |
| ει | i (or ei) | εἰκών, icon<br>δείκνυμι, deictic |
| ευ | eu, before a vowel ev | εὐ+φημί, euphemism<br>εὐαγγέλιον, evangel |
| οι | e (or oe) | οἰκουμενικός, ecumenical (also oecumenical) |
| ου | u | οὐ+τόπος, Utopia |
| (final) ια | y | εὐλογία, eulogy |

A few observations concerning the most efficient ways in which to use the following word lists will not be out of place. The usual and time-tested procedure is to concentrate on a Greek word and to repeat it to oneself over and over again with the English definition. In doing so one should be careful always to put the stress on the syllable of the

[1] In general when a Greek word has entered English through Latin it has *c* for kappa; when it has come direct, it has *k*.

Greek word which carries the accent mark. Otherwise, if, for instance, ἀδελφός be pronounced *a′del-fos* today, and *a-del′fos* tomorrow, and *a-del-fos′* at another time, the labor of learning the one Greek word is practically tripled.

Of great importance in the proper pronunciation of Greek words is a knowledge of the rules governing their division into syllables. These principles are simple. There are as many syllables in a Greek word as separate vowels or diphthongs. (1) A single consonant standing between two vowels in one word belongs with the second vowel, as ἀ-γά-πη. (2) A group of consonants that can begin a word (such combinations may be seen in a lexicon), and a group formed by a consonant followed by μ or ν, belongs with the second vowel. (3) A group of consonants that cannot begin a word is divided between two syllables, as ἐλ-πίς, ἀ-μαρ-τά-νω. Doubled consonants are divided, as θά-λασ-σα. (4) Compound words divide at the point of union, as εἰσ-φέρω, συν-έχω.

An exceedingly helpful method of learning a foreign language is to write the unfamiliar words. Indeed, according to the author of a popular treatise on the study of languages, this method ought to be practiced by every one learning a new language. Frederick Bodmer declares, 'Pen (or pencil) and paper are essential help. We are most apt to forget what we take in by ear, least likely to forget what we learn by touch. No one who has learned to swim or cycle forgets the trick of doing so.'[1] Most students discover that the effort of writing helps to fix their attention on the task at hand and thus impresses the new words more firmly in their memory. It is recommended that, in order to gain the greatest benefit from the following word lists, the student utilize both the oral and the written disciplines. Moreover, in addition to memorizing lists of words, the highest degree of proficiency in translating the New Testament can be attained only if long sections of the Greek text are read, preferably aloud.

In counting the frequency of Greek words in the New Testament, the author utilized W. F. Moulton and A. S. Geden's *Concordance to the Greek Testament*, 2nd edn. (Edinburgh, 1899). It may be mentioned that Moulton and Geden's orthography follows that of Westcott and Hort in their edition of the Greek New Testament.

---

[1] *The Loom of Language* (New York, 1944), p. 28.

The definitions have been purposely kept brief and pointed, yet it is hoped that no denotation which occurs with any degree of frequency has been neglected. For further information concerning various connotations and nuances of meaning, the following standard lexicons may be consulted.

## SELECTED BIBLIOGRAPHY OF GREEK LEXICONS

ABBOTT-SMITH, G., *A Manual Greek Lexicon of the New Testament* (3rd edn., Edinburgh, 1937).

Reasonably complete and not unwieldy, but does not make full use of new material.

ARNDT, WILLIAM F., and GINGRICH, F. WILBUR, *A Greek–English Lexicon of the New Testament and other early Christian Literature*, a translation and adaptation of Walter Bauer's *Griechisch-Deutsches Wörterbuch zu den Schriften des Neuen Testament usw.*, 4te Aufl., Berlin, 1949–52 (Chicago and Cambridge, 1957).

Best of New Testament lexicons, with rich bibliographical data. The 5th edition of Bauer's Greek–German lexicon was published in 1958.

GINGRICH, F. WILBUR, *Shorter Lexicon of the Greek New Testament* (Chicago and London, 1965).

A condensation of the Bauer–Arndt–Gingrich lexicon, without bibliographical data.

KITTEL, GERHARD (ed.), *Theologisches Wörterbuch zum Neuen Testament*, 8 vols. (Stuttgart, 1933–  ); English trans. by Geoffrey W. Bromiley, *Theological Dictionary of the New Testament* (Grand Rapids, 1964–  ).

Combines strict philological method with theological insight; an unparalleled source of information. Vols. 5 ff. are edited by Gerhard Friedrich.

LAMPE, G. W. H.,(ed.), *A Patristic Greek Lexicon*, fascicles 1–5 (Oxford, 1961–8).

The authoritative work in its field. Useful in tracing the early history of the exegesis of New Testament words and passages.

LIDDELL, H. G., and SCOTT, R., *A Greek–English Lexicon*, new edn., revised and augmented throughout by H. S. Jones, assisted by R. McKenzie (Oxford, 1925–40).

The standard lexicon of Classical Greek. A *Supplement*, edited by E. A. Barber, with the assistance of P. Maas, M. Scheller, and M. L. West (Oxford, 1968), incorporates addenda and corrigenda.

5

MOULTON, J. H., and MILLIGAN, G., *The Vocabulary of the Greek Testament Illustrated from the Papyri and Other Non-Literary Sources* (London, 1914–29; one vol. edn., 1930).

Defines only those words on which the editors found fresh information in the papyri and other non-literary sources; unsurpassed in its field.

NEWMAN, BARCLAY M., Jr., *A Concise Greek–English Dictionary of the New Testament* (New York, 1971).

A companion volume to the United Bible Societies' edition of the Greek New Testament.

PREISIGKE, FRIEDRICH, *Wörterbuch der griechischen Papyrusurkunden mit Einschluß der griechischen Inschriften, Aufschriften, Ostraka, Mumienschilder, usw., aus Ägypten*, 3 vols. (Berlin, 1925–31).

A general lexicon of the Greek papyri. A new edition is appearing as vols. 4 ff. (1944– ).

PRING, J. T., *The Oxford Dictionary of Modern Greek (Greek–English)* (Oxford, 1965).

SOUTER, ALEXANDER, *A Pocket Lexicon to the Greek New Testament* (Oxford, 1916).

Fresh, vivid definitions; its faults are those of extreme brevity and lack of helps for locating forms.

ZORELL, FRANCISCUS, *Lexicon Graecum Novi Testamenti*, 3rd edn. (Paris, 1961).

A useful Greek to Latin lexicon by a capable Jesuit scholar.

# FREQUENCY WORD LISTS

| Words occurring: | | | Words occurring: | | |
|---|---|---|---|---|---|
| more than 500 times, | pp. | 7–8 | 25 times, | pp. | 23–24 |
| 201 to 500 times, | pp. | 8–10 | 24 times, | p. | 24 |
| 151 to 200 times, | pp. | 10–11 | 23 times, | pp. | 24–25 |
| 121 to 150 times, | pp. | 11–12 | 22 times, | p. | 25 |
| 101 to 120 times, | pp. | 12–13 | 21 times, | pp. | 25–26 |
| 91 to 100 times, | p. | 13 | 20 times, | p. | 26 |
| 81 to 90 times, | pp. | 13–14 | 19 times, | p. | 27 |
| 71 to 80 times, | pp. | 14–15 | 18 times, | pp. | 27–28 |
| 61 to 70 times, | p. | 15 | 17 times, | pp. | 28–29 |
| 56 to 60 times, | p. | 16 | 16 times, | pp. | 29–30 |
| 50 to 55 times, | pp. | 16–17 | 15 times, | pp. | 30–32 |
| 46 to 49 times, | pp. | 17–18 | 14 times, | pp. | 32–33 |
| 42 to 45 times, | p. | 18 | 13 times, | pp. | 33–34 |
| 38 to 41 times, | pp. | 18–19 | 12 times, | pp. | 34–36 |
| 34 to 37 times, | pp. | 19–20 | 11 times, | pp. | 36–38 |
| 32 or 33 times, | pp. | 20–21 | 10 times, | pp. | 38–40 |
| 30 or 31 times, | pp. | 21–22 | | | |
| 28 or 29 times, | p. | 22 | | | |
| 26 or 27 times, | pp. | 22–23 | | | |

## WORDS OCCURRING MORE THAN 500 TIMES

ἄνθρωπος, -ου, ὁ, *a man* (*anthropo*logy)

ἀπό, with the gen., *from* (*apo*stasy, standing [στῆναι] off from)

αὐτός, -ή, -ό, *himself, herself, itself, same; he, she, it* (*auto*soterism, the doctrine that man is saved by his own efforts or character)

γάρ, *for*

γίνομαι, *I become, am*

δέ, *but, and*

διά, with the gen., *through*; with the acc., *on account of* (*dia*meter, measure across or through)

ἐγώ, *I* (*ego*tism)

εἰμί, *I am*

εἶπον, *I said* (cf. *epic*)

7

εἰς, with the acc., *into* (*eis*egesis, faulty interpretation of a text by read-
ing into it one's own ideas)

ἐκ, ἐξ, with the gen., *out of, from* (*ec*stasy, state of being [literally,
standing, στῆναι] out of one's senses; *ex*odus, a going [literally, a way,
ὁδός] out)

ἐν, with the dat., *in* (*en*thusiast, one possessed or inspired by a god
[ἔνθεος])

ἐπί, with the gen., *over, on, at the time of*; with the dat., *on the basis of, at*;
with the acc., *on, to, against* (*epi*dermis, upon the skin [δέρμα])

ἔρχομαι, *I come, go*

ἔχω, *I have, hold*

θεός, -οῦ, ὁ, *a god, God* (*theo*logy)

ἵνα, *in order that, that*

καί, *and, even, also*

κατά, with the gen., *down from, against*; with the acc., *according to,
throughout, during* (*cata*clysm, a washing down or against)

κύριος, -ου, ὁ, *a lord, the Lord*

λέγω, *I say, speak* (all words ending in -*ologue* or -*ology*)

μή, *not, lest*

ὁ, ἡ, τό, *the*

ὅς, ἥ, ὅ, *who, which*

ὅτι, *that, because*

οὗτος, αὕτη, τοῦτο, *this; he, her, it*

οὐ, οὐκ, οὐχ, *not* (*u*topia, no place [τόπος])

πᾶς, πᾶσα, πᾶν, *every, all* (*Pan*-American)

ποιέω, *I do, make* (*poem*; pharmaco*poeia*, making of drugs)

πρός, with the acc., *to, towards, with* (*pro*selyte, one who has come [root
of ἐλθεῖν] to another religion)

σύ, *thou*

τίς, τί, *who? what? which? why?*

τις, τι *someone, something, a certain one, a certain thing, anyone, anything*

ὡς, *as, that, how, about*


WORDS OCCURRING 201 TO 500 TIMES

ἅγιος, -α, -ον, *holy*; plural as a noun, *saints* (*Hagio*grapha, books of the
Hebrew Scriptures not included under Law and Prophets)

ἀδελφός, -οῦ, ὁ, *brother* (Phil*adelphia*, [city of] brotherly love [φιλία])

ἀκούω, *I hear* (*acoustics*)

8

ἀλλά, but, except

ἀνήρ, ἀνδρός, ὁ, a man (polyandry, having many husbands)

ἀποκρίνομαι, I answer

γῆ, γῆς, ἡ, the earth (geopolitics)

γινώσκω, I come to know, learn, know, realize

γυνή, γυναικός, ἡ, a woman, wife (misogynist, a woman-hater [μισέω])

δίδωμι, I give (antidote)

δύναμαι, I am powerful, able (cf. dynamite)

ἐάν, if

ἑαυτοῦ, of himself

εἰ, if

εἶδον, I saw (idea)

εἷς, μία, ἕν, one (henotheism, belief in one God without asserting that he is the only God)

ἐκεῖνος, -η, -ο, that

ἐξέρχομαι, I go out

ἤ, or

ἡμέρα, -ας, ἡ, a day (ephemeral, for [ἐφ᾿ (= ἐπί)] a day)

θέλω, I will, wish, desire (Monothelite, one who holds that Christ has but one will, the divine; condemned by the Sixth General Council, A.D. 680)

λαλέω, I speak (cf. glossolalia, the gift of speaking in tongues [1 Cor. 14])

λαμβάνω, I take, receive (epilepsy, a taking or seizing upon)

λόγος, -ου, ὁ, a word, the Word (logic)

μαθητής, -οῦ, ὁ, a disciple

μετά, with the gen., with; with the acc., after (metaphysics, beyond or after [Aristotle's treatise on] physics)

οἶδα, I know

ὄνομα, -ατος, τό, a name (onomatopoeia, making [ποιεῖν] a name or word [in imitation of natural sounds], as 'buzz')

οὐδείς, οὐδεμία, οὐδέν, no one, none, nothing, no

οὖν, therefore, then, accordingly

οὐρανός, -οῦ, ὁ, heaven (the planet Uranus; the element uranium)

οὕτως, thus

πατήρ, πατρός, ὁ, father (akin to paternal)

περί, with the gen., concerning, about; with the acc., around (perimeter, measure around)

πιστεύω, I have faith (in), believe

πίστις, -εως, ἡ, faith, belief, trust

9

πνεῦμα, -ατος, τό, a spirit, the Spirit (pneumatology, the doctrine of the Holy Spirit)

πολύς, πολλή, πολύ, much; plural, many (polytheism)

υἱός, -οῦ, ὁ, a son

ὑπό, with the gen., by; with the acc., under (hypodermic, under the skin [δέρμα])

WORDS OCCURRING 151 TO 200 TIMES

ἄγγελος, -ου, ὁ, a messenger, an angel (angel)

ἁμαρτία, -ας, ἡ, a sin, sin (hamartiology, the doctrine of sin)

ἄν, an untranslatable word, the effect of which is to make a statement contingent which would otherwise be definite

βασιλεία, -ας, ἡ, a kingdom

γράφω, I write (palaeography, the study of ancient [παλαιός] writing)

δόξα, -ης, ἡ, glory (doxology)

ἔθνος, -ους, τό, a nation; plural, the Gentiles (ethnology)

εἰσέρχομαι, I go or come in or into, enter

ἔργον, -ου, τό, work (energy)

ἐσθίω, I eat (akin to edible)

εὑρίσκω, I find (heuristic, the method in education by which a pupil is set to find out things for himself; eureka, 'I have found [it]!'—Archimedes

ἰδού, see! behold!

ἵστημι, I cause to stand, I stand (akin to stand)

καθώς, as, even as

καρδία, -ας, ἡ, the heart (cardiac)

κόσμος, ου, ὁ, the world (cosmic, cosmos)

μέγας, μεγάλη, μέγα, large, great (megaphone; omega [literally, great 'o'])

μέν, postpositive particle, on the one hand, indeed (often it is better left untranslated and its presence shown by stress of the voice and by translating a following δέ by 'but')

νεκρός, -ά, -όν, dead; as a noun, a dead body, a corpse (necropolis, city of the dead, a cemetery)

νόμος, -ου, ὁ, a law, the Law (Deuteronomy, the second [statement of the] law)

ὅστις, ἥτις, ὅτι, whoever, whichever, whatever

ὄχλος, -ου, ὁ, a crowd, multitude (ochlocracy, mob-rule)

παρά, with the gen. from; with the dat., beside, in the presence of; with the acc., *alongside of* (*para*graph, originally, in manuscripts, a stroke or line drawn in the margin *beside* the column of writing to mark the division of sections)

πόλις, -εως, ἡ, *a city* (Nea*polis*, 'New City,' Acts 16: 11; Constantino*ple*, Constantine's City)

πορεύομαι, *I go, proceed*

τε, (an enclitic connective particle, weaker in force than καί), *and*

τότε, *then, at that time*

ὑπέρ, with the gen., *in behalf of*; with the acc., *above* (*hyper*critical)

χάρις, -ιτος, ἡ, *grace* (*Charissa*, [girl's name])

χείρ, χειρός, ἡ, *a hand* (*chiro*graphy, handwriting)

### WORDS OCCURRING 121 TO 150 TIMES

ἀγαπάω, *I love*

αἰών, -ῶνος, ὁ, *an age* (*aeon*)

ἄλλος, -η, -o, *other, another* (*alle*gory, description of one thing under the image of another)

ἀμήν, *verily, truly, amen* (*amen*)

ἀποστέλλω, *I send* (with a commission) (cf. *Apostle*)

ἀρχιερεύς, -έως, ὁ, *chief priest, high priest*

ἀφίημι, *I let go, permit, forgive* (*aphesis*, the gradual loss of a short unaccented initial vowel, as 'squire' for 'esquire')

βάλλω, *I throw, put* (*ballistics*, the science of the motion of projectiles)

βλέπω, *I see*

δοῦλος, -ου, ὁ, *a slave*

δύο, *two* (*dyad*)

ἐγείρω, *I raise up*

ἕως, *until*; with the gen., *as far as*

ζάω, *I live*

ζωή, -ῆς, ἡ, *life* (*Zoe* [girl's name])

καλέω, *I call, name, invite*

λαός, -οῦ, ὁ, *a people* (*laity*)

νῦν, *now*

ὅταν, *whenever*

οὐδέ, *and not, not even, neither, nor*

πάλιν, *again* (*palim*psest, a manuscript which has been used again, the earlier writing having been erased [ψῆν, to scrape or erase])

παραδίδωμι, *I hand over, betray*

προφήτης, -ου, ὁ, a prophet (prophet)

σάρξ, σαρκός, ἡ, flesh (sarcophagus, a [stone] coffin which 'eats' [φαγεῖν] the contents)

σύν, with the dat., with (syntax, sentence construction, involving grammatical arrangement [τάσσειν] of words with one another)

σῶμα, -ατος, τό, a body (somatic)

φωνή, -ῆς, a sound, voice (phonetic)

## WORDS OCCURRING 101 TO 120 TIMES

ἀγαθός, -ή, -όν, good (Agatha)

ἀγάπη, -ης, ἡ, love

ἀλήθεια, -ας, ἡ, truth

ἀνίστημι, I cause to rise; I arise

ἀπέρχομαι, I depart

ἀποθνῄσκω, I die

βασιλεύς, -έως, ὁ, a king (Basil)

δεῖ, it is necessary

δύναμις, -εως, ἡ, power (dynamite)

ἐκκλησία, -ας, ἡ, assembly, congregation, a church, the Church (ecclesiastic)

ἐξουσία, -ας, ἡ, authority

ζητέω, I seek

θάνατος, -ου, ὁ, death (thanatopsis, a view of, or meditation on, death)

ἴδιος, -α, -ον, one's own (idiosyncrasy)

κρίνω, I judge, decide (critic)

μέλλω, I am about to

μένω, I remain (akin to permanent)

ὁδός, -οῦ, ἡ, a way, road, journey, (anode, cathode, electrical terminals)

οἶκος, -ου, ὁ, a house (economy, household management)

ὅλος, -η, -ον, whole (holocaust)

ὁράω, I see (cf. panorama [πᾶν, all + ὅραμα, a view])

ὅσος, -η, -ον, as great as, as many as

ὅτε, when

παρακαλέω, I beseech, exhort, console (Paraclete, the Comforter, Helper, Advocate, or Counselor)

πῶς, how?

σῴζω, I save (in biochemistry, sozin, any defensive protein in the animal body)

ψυχή, -ῆς, ἡ, soul, life, self (all words beginning with psycho-)

ὥρα, -ας, ἡ, an hour (horoscope, prediction based on the observation of the hour of one's birth)

αἷμα, -ατος, τό, blood (anaemia, without blood; haemoglobin)

αἴρω, I take up, take away

ἀλλήλων, of one another (parallel, beside [παρ'] one another)

ἄρτος, -ου, ὁ, bread, a loaf

γεννάω, I beget (cf. hydrogen, so called as being considered the generator of water [ὕδωρ])

διδάσκω, I teach (cf. didactic)

δικαιοσύνη, -ης, ἡ, righteousness

εἰρήνη, -ης, ἡ, peace (Irene)

ἐκεῖ, there

ἐρῶ, I shall say

ἕτερος, -α, -ον, other, another, different (heterodoxy)

θάλασσα, -ης, ἡ, the sea (thalassic)

καλός, -ή, -όν, beautiful, good (kaleidoscope [εἶδος, form + σκοπεῖν, to behold])

οἰκία, -ας, ἡ, a house

οὔτε, neither, nor

ὀφθαλμός, -οῦ, ὁ, an eye (ophthalmology)

περιπατέω, I walk; I live (peripatetics)

πούς, ποδός, ὁ, a foot (podium)

πρῶτος, -η, -ον, first (all words beginning with proto-)

τέκνον, -ου, τό, a child

τίθημι, I place (cf. antithesis)

τόπος, -ου, ὁ, a place (topography, topic)

φοβέομαι, I fear (cf. phobia)

ἀκολουθέω, I follow (cf. acolyte, the assistant who carries the wine and water and the lights at the celebration of the Mass, attending or following the priest)

ἀναβαίνω, I go up (Anabasis)

ἀπόλλυμι, I destroy; middle, I perish (Apollyon, the angel of the bottomless pit, Rev. 9:11)

ἄρχω, I rule; in the New Testament almost always middle, I begin
ἕκαστος, -η, -ον, each
ἐκβάλλω, I cast out
ἐνώπιον, with the gen., before
ἔτι, still, yet, even
κάθημαι, I sit
καιρός, -οῦ, ὁ, time, an appointed time, season
μηδείς, μηδεμία, μηδέν, no one
μήτηρ, μητρός, ἡ, a mother (akin to maternal)
ὅπου, where, whither
πίπτω, I fall
πληρόω, I fill, fulfill
προσέρχομαι, I come to
προσεύχομαι, I pray
ὥστε, so that

## WORDS OCCURRING 71 TO 80 TIMES

αἰτέω, I ask
ἀνοίγω, I open
ἀποκτείνω, I kill
ἀπόστολος, -ον, ὁ, an Apostle (Apostle)
βαπτίζω, I baptize (baptize)
δίκαιος, -α, -ον, right, just, righteous
δώδεκα, twelve (dodecagon)
ἐμός, ἐμή, ἐμόν, my, mine
ἑπτά, seven (heptagon)
εὐαγγέλιον, -ον, τό, good news (of the coming of the Messiah), the
Gospel (Evangel)
ἱερόν, -οῦ, τό, a temple (cf. hierarchy)
καταβαίνω, I go down
κεφαλή, -ῆς, ἡ, head (cephalic)
μᾶλλον, more, rather
μαρτυρέω, I bear witness, testify (cf. martyr)
πέμπω, I send
πίνω, I drink (cf. potion)
πονηρός, -ά, -όν, evil
πρόσωπον, -ον, τό, face (prosopography, description of the face or
personal appearance)

14

πῦρ, πυρός, τό, fire (pyre)
σημεῖον, -ου, τό, a sign (cf. semaphore, bearing [φέρειν] a sign)
στόμα, -ατος, τό, a mouth (stomach)
τηρέω, I keep
ὕδωρ, ὕδατος, τό, water (hydrophobia; dropsy [formerly hydropsy])
ὑπάγω, I depart
φῶς, φωτός, τό, light (photography, writing [γράφειν] with light)
χαίρω, I rejoice


WORDS OCCURRING 61 TO 70 TIMES

ἀγαπητός, -ή, -όν, beloved
ἄγω, I lead
αἰώνιος, -ον, eternal (aeonian)
ἀπολύω, I release
γραμματεύς, -έως, ὁ, a scribe (cf. grammatical)
δαιμόνιον, -ου, τό, a demon (demon)
δοκέω, I think; seem (Docetism, the early heresy that Christ's body was
    phantasmal or of celestial substance which merely seemed human)
ἐντολή, -ῆς, ἡ, a commandment
ἔξω, without; with the gen., outside
θέλημα, -ατος, τό, will (Monothelite, one who holds that Christ had
    but one will, the divine; condemned by the Sixth General Council,
    A.D. 680)
ἱμάτιον, -ου, τό, a garment
καρπός, -οῦ, ὁ, fruit
κηρύσσω, I proclaim (as a herald, κῆρυξ), preach
νύξ, νυκτός, ἡ, night
ὄρος, ὄρους, τό, a mountain (orology, the scientific study of mountains)
πιστός, -ή, όν, faithful, believing
πλοῖον, -ου, τό, a boat
πρεσβύτερος, -α, -ον, elder (presbyter)
ῥῆμα -ατος, τό, a word (cf. rhetoric)
σάββατον, -ου, τό, the Sabbath (Sabbath)
συνάγω, I gather together (synagogue)
τρεῖς, τρία, three (triad)
φέρω, I carry, bear, lead (Christopher, bearing Christ)
ὧδε, hither, here

15

ἀρχή, -ῆς, ἡ, a beginning (archaic)

ἀσπάζομαι, I greet, salute

δέχομαι, I receive

διδάσκαλος, -ον, ὁ, a teacher (cf. didactic)

δοξάζω, I glorify (cf. doxology)

ἐπερωτάω, I ask, question, demand of

ἐρωτάω, I ask, request, entreat

ἤδη, now, already

θρόνος, -ον, ὁ, a throne (throne)

κράζω, I cry out

λοιπός, -ή, -όν, remaining; as a noun, the rest; as an adverb, for the rest, henceforth

μέσος, -η, -ον, middle, in the midst (Mesopotamia, in the midst of the rivers [Tigris and Euphrates])

οὐχί (strengthened form of οὐ), not

πλείων, -ονος, larger, more (pleonasm)

προσκυνέω, I worship

συναγωγή, -ῆς, ἡ, a synagogue (synagogue)

τοιοῦτος, -αύτη, -οῦτον and -οῦτο, such

ὑπάρχω, I am, exist; τὰ ὑπάρχοντα, one's belongings

φημί, I say

χαρά, -ᾶς, ἡ, joy, delight

ἄχρι, ἄχρις, with the gen., as far as, up to; as a conjunction, until

γλῶσσα, -ης, ἡ, a tongue, language (glossolalia, the gift of speaking [cf. λαλεῖν] in tongues, 1 Cor. 14)

γραφή, -ῆς, ἡ, a writing, Scripture (Hagiographa, books of the Hebrew Scriptures not included under Law and Prophets)

δεξιός, -ά, -όν, right (opp. left) (akin to dexterous)

διό, wherefore

ἐλπίς, -ίδος, ἡ, hope

ἐπαγγελία, -ας, ἡ, a promise

ἔσχατος, -η, -ον, last (eschatology)

εὐαγγελίζω, I bring good news, preach good tidings (the Gospel) (evangelize)

εὐθύς, straightway, immediately

θεωρέω, *I look at, behold* (*theorem*; *theory*)
λίθος, -ου, ὁ, *a stone* (mono*lith*; *litho*graph)
μακάριος, -α, -ον, *blessed, happy* (*macarism*, a beatitude)
μηδέ, *but not, nor, not even*
μόνος, -η, -ον, *alone, only* (*mono*logue)
ὅπως, *in order that, that*
παιδίον, -ου, τό, *an infant, child*
παραβολή, -ῆς, ἡ, *a parable* (*parable*)
πείθω, *I persuade*
σοφία, -ας, ἡ, *wisdom* (philo*sophy*)
χρόνος, -ου, ὁ, *time* (*chrono*logy)

## WORDS OCCURRING 46 TO 49 TIMES

ἁμαρτωλός, -όν, *sinful*; as a noun, *a sinner*
ἀπαγγέλλω, *I announce, report*
ἀποδίδωμι, *I give back, pay*; middle, *I sell*
ἄρα, *then, therefore*
ἔμπροσθεν, with the gen., *in front of, before*
ἔρημος, -ον, *solitary, deserted*; as a noun, ἡ ἔρημος, *the desert, wilderness* (*hermit*)
ἔτος, -ους, τό, *a year* (the *Etesian* winds in the Mediterranean region blow *annually*)
καθίζω, *I seat, sit* (cf. *cathedral*, properly, the church which contains the bishop's chair or seat)
κακός, -ή, -όν, *bad, evil* (*caco*phony, discord)
κρατέω, *I grasp* (cf. pluto*cratic*, grasping wealth [πλοῦτος])
κρίσις, -εως, ἡ, *judgment* (*crisis*)
μικρός, -ά, -όν, *small, little* (*micro*scope; *omicron*, little 'o')
οὐκέτι, *no longer*
παραλαμβάνω, *I receive*
ποῦ, *where? whither?*
πρό, with the gen., *before* (*pro*logue)
προσφέρω, *I bring to, offer*
σπείρω, *I sow*
σωτηρία, -ας, ἡ, *salvation* (*soterio*logy)
τρίτος, -η, -ον, *third*
τυφλός, -ή, -όν, *blind* (*typhlosis*, medical term for blindness)
φανερόω, *I make manifest*

17

φόβος, -ου, ὁ, fear, terror (phobia)
φυλακή, -ῆς, ἡ, a guard, a prison, a watch
χρεία, -ας, ἡ, a need

### WORDS OCCURRING 42 TO 45 TIMES

ἁμαρτάνω, I sin (cf. hamartiology, the doctrine of sin)
ἀνάστασις, -εως, ἡ, resurrection (Anastasia [girl's name])
ἅπας, -ασα, -αν, all
γενεά, -ᾶς, ἡ, a generation (genealogy)
δεύτερος, -α, -ον, second (Deuteronomy, the second [statement of the]
    law)
δέω, I bind (diadem, literally, something bound around or across)
διώκω, I pursue, persecute
ἐγγίζω, I come near
ἐπιγινώσκω, I come to know, recognize
εὐλογέω, I bless (eulogize)
θαυμάζω, I marvel, wonder at (cf. thaumaturge, a worker of miracles or
    wonders)
θεραπεύω, I heal (therapeutic)
θηρίον, -ου, τό, a wild beast (theriomorphic, having animal form; as,
    theriomorphic gods)
θλῖψις, -εως, ἡ, tribulation
κατοικέω, I inhabit, dwell
λύω, I loose (cf. analysis, a resolving or unloosing into simple elements)
μέρος, -ους, τό, a part (in biology, pentamerous, of five parts)
ναός, -οῦ, ὁ, a temple
ὅμοιος, -α, -ον, like (Homoiousian, one holding that Father and Son in
    the Godhead are of like [but not the same] substance; a semi-Arian)
σεαυτοῦ, of thyself
σήμερον, today
σπέρμα, -ατος, τό, a seed (sperm)
σταυρόω, I crucify
τιμή, -ῆς, ἡ, honor, price (cf. Timothy, honoring God)
φωνέω, I call (phonetic)

### WORDS OCCURRING 38 TO 41 TIMES

ἄξιος, -α, -ον, worthy (axiom; in philosophy and psychology, axiological,
    pertaining to the science of values)

18

ἅπτομαι, I touch
διέρχομαι, I pass through
δικαιόω, I justify, pronounce righteous
ἐπιθυμία, -ας, ἡ, eager desire, passion
ἐπιτίθημι, I lay upon
ἐργάζομαι, I work (cf. energy)
ἑτοιμάζω, I prepare
εὐχαριστέω, I give thanks (Eucharist)
θύρα, -ας, ἡ, a door
ἱκανός, -ή, -όν, sufficient, able, considerable
καινός, -ή, -όν, new
κλαίω, I weep
λογίζομαι, I account, reckon (cf. logic)
μισέω, I hate (misogynist, a woman-hater)
μνημεῖον, -ου, τό, a tomb, monument
οἰκοδομέω, I build, edify
ὀλίγος, -η, -ον, little, few (oligarchy, rule by the few)
οὐαί, woe! alas!
πάντοτε, always
παραγίνομαι, I come, arrive
παρίστημι, I am present, stand by
πάσχω, I suffer
περισσεύω, I abound, am rich
πλανάω, I lead astray (planet, to the ancients, an apparently 'wandering'
    celestial body)
πράσσω, I do, perform (praxis, practice, as opposed to theory)
πρόβατον, -ου, τό, a sheep
τέλος, -ους, τό, end (teleology, in philosophy, the view that develop-
    ments are due to the purpose or design [end] that is served by them)
χωρίς, with the gen., without, apart from


WORDS OCCURRING 34 TO 37 TIMES

ἀγρός, -οῦ, ὁ, a field (akin to agrarian)
ἄρτι, now, just now
ἄρχων, -οντος, ὁ, a ruler (monarch, sole [μόνος] ruler)
ἀσθενέω, I am weak
βλασφημέω, I revile, blaspheme (blaspheme)
βούλομαι, I wish, determine (akin to volition)

19

διάβολος, -ον, *slanderous, accusing falsely*; as a noun, *the Accuser, the Devil* (*diabolical*)

διακονέω, *I wait upon* (especially at table), *serve* (generally), *minister* (cf. *deacon*)

ἐκπορεύομαι, *I go out*

ἐμαυτοῦ, *of myself*

ἐπιστρέφω, *I turn to, return*

εὐθέως, *immediately*

καλῶς, *well*

μαρτυρία, -ας, ἡ, *a testimony, evidence* (cf. *martyrdom*)

μάρτυς, -υρος, ὁ, *a witness* (*martyr*)

μετανοέω, *I repent*

ὀπίσω, *behind, after*; with the gen., *behind, after* (cf. *opistho*graph, a manuscript written upon both the back and the front, Rev. 5:1)

ὀργή, ῆς, ἡ, *anger*

οὖς, ὠτός, τό, *an ear* (*oto*logy)

ὀφείλω, *I owe, ought*

πειράζω, *I test, tempt, attempt*

πέντε, *five* (*Penta*teuch)

περιτομή, -ῆς, ἡ, *circumcision*

προσευχή, -ῆς, ἡ, *prayer*

πτωχός, -ή, -όν, *poor*; as a noun, *a poor man*

τέσσαρες, -ων, *four* (the Dia*tessaron* of Tatian, a harmony of the four Gospels made about A.D. 170; literally, through [*the*] *four*)

ὑποστρέφω, *I return*

ὑποτάσσω, *I subject, put in subjection* (in grammar, *hypotaxis*, subordination of clauses)

ὥσπερ, *just as, even as*


WORDS OCCURRING 32 OR 33 TIMES

ἀναγινώσκω, *I read*

ἀρνέομαι, *I deny*

βιβλίον, -ου, τό, *a book* (*Bible*)

δεικνύω or δείκνυμι, *I show* (in logic, apo*deictic*, of clear demonstration)

διαθήκη, -ης, ἡ, *a covenant*

διακονία, -ας, ἡ, *waiting at table*, (in a wider sense) *service, ministry* (*diaconate*)

δυνατός, -ή, -όν, *powerful, possible* (cf. *dynamite*)

20

ἐγγύς, near
ἔξεστι, it is lawful
ἐχθρός, -ά, -όν, hating; as a noun, an enemy
ἥλιος, -ου, ὁ, the sun (helium)
ἱερεύς, -έως, ὁ, a priest (hierarchy)
καυχάομαι, I boast
μέλος, -ους, τό, a member
μήτε, neither, nor
οἶνος, -ου, ὁ, wine
πλῆθος, -ους, τό, a multitude (cf. plethora)
ποῖος, -α, -ον, what sort of? what?
ποτήριον, -ου, τό, a cup
συνέρχομαι, I come together
ὑπομονή, -ῆς, ἡ, steadfast endurance
φυλάσσω, I guard (cf. prophylactic)

## WORDS OCCURRING 30 OR 31 TIMES

ἀγοράζω, I buy (cf. agora, the market place)
ἀκάθαρτος, -ον, unclean
ἄνεμος, -ου, ὁ, a wind (anemone; anemometer)
ἀρνίον, -ου, τό, a lamb
γε, indeed, at least, really, even
διδαχή, -ῆς, ἡ, teaching (cf. didactic)
ἐλεέω, I have mercy (cf. eleemosynary; alms)
ἐλπίζω, I hope
ἐπικαλέω, I call, name; middle, I invoke, appeal to
ἐπιτιμάω, I rebuke, warn
καθαρίζω, I cleanse (catharize)
ναί, yea, truly, yes
ὁμοίως, likewise
παραγγέλλω, I command, charge
παρέρχομαι, I pass by, pass away; I arrive
παρρησία, -ας, ἡ, boldness (of speech), confidence
πλήν, however, but, only; with the gen., except
σκανδαλίζω, I cause to stumble (scandalize)
σκότος, -ους, τό, darkness (scotoscope, a field-glass for seeing by night)
συνείδησις, -εως, ἡ, conscience
φαίνω, I shine, appear (phantom; phenomenon)

φεύγω, *I flee* (cf. *fugitive*)
φυλή, -ῆς, ἡ, *a tribe* (in zoology, *phylum*, one of the large fundamental divisions of the animal kingdom)

## WORDS OCCURRING 28 OR 29 TIMES

ἀληθινός, -ή, -όν, *true*
γαμέω, *I marry* (in biology, *gamete*, a matured germ cell)
γνῶσις, -εως, ἡ, *wisdom* (*gnosis*; *Gnostic*)
διάκονος, -ου, ὁ and ἡ, *a servant, administrator, deacon* (*deacon*)
ἐνδύω, *I put on, clothe*
ἐπεί, *when, since*
ἡγέομαι, *I am chief; I think, regard*
θυσία, -ας, ἡ, *a sacrifice*
ἴδε, *see! behold!*
ἰσχυρός, -ά, -όν, *strong*
ἰσχύω, *I am strong, able*
κρίμα, -ατος, τό, *judgment* (cf. *crisis*)
μάχαιρα, -ης, ἡ, *a sword*
μισθός, -οῦ, ὁ, *wages, reward*
μυστήριον, -ου, τό, *a mystery* (*mystery*)
οὔπω, *not yet*
παράκλησις, -εως, ἡ, *an exhortation, consolation* (cf. *Paraclete*, the Comforter, Helper, Advocate, or Counselor)
πάσχα, indeclinable, τό, *a passover* (*paschal*)
πλούσιος, -α, -ον, *rich* (cf. *pluto*cratic)
πόθεν, *whence?*
ποτέ, *at some time, once, ever*
προσκαλέομαι, *I summon*
προφητεύω, *I prophesy* (cf. *prophet*)
τελέω, *I finish, fulfill* (cf. *teleology*, in philosophy, the view that developments are due to the purpose or design [τέλος] that is served by them)
φίλος, -η, -ον, *loving*; as a noun, *a friend* (biblio*phile*)

## WORDS OCCURRING 26 OR 27 TIMES

ἁγιάζω, *I sanctify* (cf. *hagio*latry, the worship of saints)
ἀδελφή, -ῆς, ἡ, *a sister*

ἀδικία, -ας, ἡ, unrighteousness
ἀληθής, -ές, true
ἀποκαλύπτω, I reveal (apocalypse)
βαστάζω, I bear, carry
ἐκεῖθεν, thence, from that place
ἔλεος, -ους, τό, pity, mercy (cf. eleemosynary; alms)
ἑορτή, -ῆς, ἡ, a feast
ἥκω, I have come
θυγάτηρ, -τρός, ἡ, a daughter
ἰάομαι, I heal (cf. pediatrics, medical care of children [παῖς, παιδός])
καταργέω, I bring to naught, abolish
κελεύω, I order
κώμη, -ης, ἡ, a village
λυπέω, I grieve
νικάω, I conquer (cf. Nicholas, victor over the people [λαός])
ὀμνύω or ὄμνυμι, I swear, take an oath
πόσος, -η, -ον, how great? how much?
σός, σή, σόν, thy, thine
σταυρός, -οῦ, ὁ, a cross
στρατιώτης, -ου, ὁ, a soldier
συνίημι, I understand
φρονέω, I think
χήρα, -ας, ἡ, a widow
χώρα, -ας, ἡ, a country (chorography, describing, or description, of districts)

WORDS OCCURRING 25 TIMES

ἀδικέω, I wrong, do wrong
ἀναβλέπω, I look up, receive sight
γνωρίζω, I make known
δέκα, ten (Decapolis, a league originally consisting of ten Greek cities, mostly SE. of the sea of Galilee)
δένδρον, -ου, τό, a tree (rhododendron, lit. rose-tree)
δουλεύω, I serve
ἕνεκα or ἕνεκεν, with the gen., on account of
καθαρός, -ά, -όν, clean (catharsis)
μανθάνω, I learn (cf. mathematics)
μήποτε, lest perchance

23

νεφέλη, -ης, ἡ, a cloud (nephelometer)
ὁμολογέω, I confess, profess
οὗ, where
πνευματικός, -ή, -όν, spiritual (pneumatic)
πορνεία, -ας, ἡ, fornication (cf. pornography)
προσέχω, I attend to, give heed to
φιλέω, I love (cf. bibliophile)

## WORDS OCCURRING 24 TIMES

ἀκοή, -ῆς, ἡ, hearing; a report
ἀναιρέω, I take up; kill
ἀσθένεια, -ας, ἡ, weakness (neurasthenia, nervous prostration)
ἀσθενής, -ές, weak (cf. neurasthenia)
διότι, because
ἐκλεκτός, -ή, -όν, chosen, elect (cf. eclecticism)
ἐπιστολή, -ῆς, ἡ, a letter (epistle)
καταλείπω, I leave
κατηγορέω, I accuse (cf. categorical)
κεῖμαι, I lie, am laid
νοῦς, νοός, ὁ, the mind (noetic)
παῖς, παιδός, ὁ and ἡ, a boy, girl, child, servant (pedagogue, literally, child-leader)
πάρειμι, I am present; I have arrived
παρουσία, -ας, ἡ, presence, coming (especially Christ's [second] coming in glory) (Parousia)
περιβάλλω, I put around, clothe
πίμπλημι, I fill
σωτήρ, -ῆρος, ὁ, Saviour (cf. soteriology)

## WORDS OCCURRING 23 TIMES

ἀμπελών, -ῶνος, ὁ, a vineyard
ἀνάγω, I lead up; middle, I put to sea, set sail
ἄπιστος, -ον, unbelieving, faithless
ἀστήρ, -έρος, ὁ, a star (aster)
αὐξάνω, I cause to grow; increase (cf. auxiliary)
γρηγορέω, I watch (Gregory)
εἰκών, -όνος, ἡ, an image (icon)

24

ἐλεύθερος, -α, -ον, *free*
ζῷον, -ου, τό, *a living creature, an animal* (*zoo*logy)
θυσιαστήριον, -ου, τό, *an altar*
κοπιάω, *I toil*
κωλύω, *I forbid, hinder*
λευκός, -ή, -όν, *white* (*leuk*emia, literally, white blood [αἷμα])
μιμνήσκομαι, *I remember* (cf. *mnemonics*)
νέος, -α, -ον, *new, young* (all words beginning with *neo-*)
πεινάω, *I hunger*
πέραν, with the gen., *beyond*
περισσός, -ή, -όν, *excessive, abundant*
σκεῦος, -ους, τό, *a vessel*; plural, *goods*
τελειόω, *I fulfill, make perfect*
χαρίζομαι, *I give freely, forgive*

## WORDS OCCURRING 22 TIMES

δέομαι, *I beseech*
δοκιμάζω, *I prove, approve*
θεάομαι, *I behold* (*theater*)
καθεύδω, *I sleep*
καθίστημι, *I set, constitute*
κατεργάζομαι, *I work out*
κοιλία, -ας, ἡ, *the belly* (stomach or intestines, or both); *womb* (*coeliac*, pertaining to the abdomen)
μετάνοια, -ας, ἡ, *repentance*
μηκέτι, *no longer*
νυνί, *now*
πληγή, -ῆς, ἡ, *a blow, wound, plague* (*plague*)
πλοῦτος, -ου, ὁ, *wealth* (*pluto*crat)
πωλέω, *I sell* (cf. mono*poly*)
στρέφω, *I turn* (*strophe*)
συνέδριον, -ου, τό, *a council, the Sanhedrin* (*Sanhedrin*)
χιλίαρχος, -ου, ὁ, *a military tribune, captain* (*chiliarch*)
ὡσεί, *as, like, about*

## WORDS OCCURRING 21 TIMES

ἀγνοέω, *I do not know* (*agnostic*)
ἀντί, with the gen., *instead of, for* (all words beginning with *anti-*)

ἀργύριον, -ον, τό, silver (in pharmacy, *Argyrol*, the trade-name of a silver-protein compound)
βασιλεύω, I reign
γένος, -ους, τό, race, kind (akin to *genus*)
διδασκαλία, -ας, ἡ, teaching
ἑκατοντάρχης (or -αρχος), -ου, ὁ, a centurion
ἐκλέγομαι, I pick out, choose (*eclectic*)
εὐδοκέω, I think it good, am well pleased with
ἐφίστημι, I stand over, come upon
θερίζω, I reap
λατρεύω, I serve, worship (cf. Mariolatry)
μνημονεύω, I remember (cf. *mnemonics*)
παράπτωμα, -ατος, τό, a trespass
πειρασμός, -οῦ, ὁ, temptation
τελώνης, -ου, ὁ, a taxgatherer
τεσσαράκοντα, indeclinable, *forty*
τιμάω, I honor (*Timothy*, honoring God)
ὑπακούω, I obey
χιλιάς, -άδος, ἡ, a thousand (*chiliasm*, millenarianism)

## WORDS OCCURRING 20 TIMES

αἰτία, -ας, ἡ, a cause, accusation (*etiology*, the investigation of causes)
ἀκροβυστία, -ας, ἡ, uncircumcision
βάπτισμα, -ατος, τό, baptism (*baptism*)
γονεύς, -έως, ὁ, a parent (cf. *gonad*)
ἐνεργέω, I work, effect (cf. *energy*)
ἐπίγνωσις, -εως, ἡ, knowledge
ἰχθύς, -ύος, ὁ, a fish (*ichthyology*)
κρύπτω, I conceal (*cryptic*)
μαρτύριον, -ου, τό, a testimony, witness, proof (cf. *martyrdom*)
ξύλον, -ου, τό, wood, tree (*xylophone*)
προάγω, I lead forth, go before
σκηνή, -ῆς, ἡ, a tent, tabernacle (*scene*)
σοφός, -ή, -όν, wise (cf. *sophomore*, literally, a wise fool [μωρός])
ὑπηρέτης, -ου, ὁ, a servant, assistant
ὑψόω, I lift up, exalt (cf. *hypsophobia*, fear of high places)

ἀπέχω, *I have received* (payment); *I am distant*
γεωργός, -οῦ, ὁ, *a farmer* (*George*)
διακρίνω, *I discriminate, judge*; middle, *I doubt*
δῶρον, -ου, τό, *a gift* (Theo*dore*, *Dorothea* [or *Dorothy*], gift of God)
ἐπαίρω, *I lift up*
ἐπάνω, *above*; with the gen., *over*
ἐπιβάλλω, *I lay upon*
ἐπιλαμβάνομαι, *I take hold of*
ἐπουράνιος, -ιον, *heavenly*
ἡγεμών, -όνος, ὁ, *a leader, a* (Roman) *governor* (cf. *hegemony*, leadership, especially of one state of a confederacy)
κοινωνία, -ας, ἡ, *fellowship*; *contribution*
κρείσσων or κρείττων, -ονος, *better*
κριτής, -οῦ, ὁ, *a judge* (*critic*)
κτίσις, -εως, ἡ, *creation, creature*
μεριμνάω, *I am anxious, distracted*
μέχρι or μέχρις, *until*; with the gen., *as far as*
νηστεύω, *I fast*
παλαιός, -ά, -όν, *old* (*palaeo*graphy)
παρατίθημι, *I set before*; middle, *I entrust*
πότε, *when?*
προφητεία, -ας, ἡ, *a prophecy* (*prophecy*)
τέλειος, -α, -ον, *complete, perfect, mature* (cf. *teleology*)
τοσοῦτος, -αύτη, -οῦτον and -οῦτο, *so great, so much*; plural, *so many*
τρέχω, *I run*

ἀληθῶς, *truly*
ἀνάγκη, -ης, ἡ, *necessity*
ἀποκάλυψις, -εως, ἡ, *a revelation* (*apocalypse*)
ἀπώλεια, -ας, ἡ, *destruction* (cf. *Apollyon*)
ἀριθμός, -οῦ, ὁ, *a number* (*arithmetic*)
βλασφημία, -ας, ἡ, *reproach, blasphemy* (*blasphemy*)
δέησις, -εως, ἡ, *an entreaty*
δεσμός, -οῦ, ὁ, *a fetter, bond*
εἰσπορεύομαι, *I enter*

ἐλέγχω, *I convict, reprove* (elenchus, a logical refutation)
ἐμβαίνω, *I embark*
ἐπιτρέπω, *I permit*
θυμός, -οῦ, ὁ, *wrath*
καταγγέλλω, *I proclaim*
κατακρίνω, *I condemn*
κατέχω, *I hold back, hold fast*
κενός, -ή, -όν, *empty, vain* (cenotaph, sepulchral monument to a person whose body is not contained in it)
κληρονομέω, *I inherit*
κοιμάομαι, *I sleep, fall asleep* (cemetery, literally, a sleeping chamber)
κόπος, -ου, ὁ, *labor, trouble*
κρυπτός, -ή, -όν, *hidden* (cryptic)
μήν, μηνός, ὁ, *a month* (menology, a calendar, especially that of the Greek Church, provided with short biographies of saints)
μήτι, interrogative particle in questions expecting a negative answer
οἰκοδομή, -ῆς, ἡ, *a building*; *edification*
παράχρημα, *immediately*
ποιμήν, -ένος, ὁ, *a shepherd* (poimenic, pertaining to pastoral theology)
πόλεμος, -ου, ὁ, *a war* (polemics)
προστίθημι, *I add, add to*
πυλών, -ῶνος, ὁ, *a vestibule, gateway* (pylon)
στέφανος, -ου, ὁ, *a crown* (Stephen)
ταράσσω, *I trouble*
τίκτω, *I give birth to*
ὑποκριτής, -οῦ, ὁ, *a hypocrite*
ὑπομένω, *I tarry*; *I endure*
φανερός, -ά, όν, *manifest*
χρύσεος, -α, -ον, contracted χρυσοῦς, -ῆ, -οῦν, *golden* (chrysanthemum, literally, golden flower)

WORDS OCCURRING 17 TIMES

ἀρέσκω, *I please*
αὐτοῦ, *of himself*
ἄφεσις, -εως, ἡ, *a sending away, remission* (aphesis, the gradual loss of a short unaccented vowel at the beginning of a word; as 'squire' for 'esquire')
βρῶμα, -ατος, τό, *food*

γάμος, -ου, ὁ, *a marriage, wedding* (bi*gamy*, double marriage; di*gamy*, second marriage after the decease of the first spouse, condemned as a sin by certain Church Fathers)

δέσμιος, -ου, ὁ, *a prisoner*

ἑκατόν, *one hundred* (*hecatomb*, great public sacrifice, properly of 100 oxen [βοῦς])

ἐξίστημι, *I amaze, am amazed*

ἐπαύριον, *on the morrow*

ἐπιμένω, *I continue*

ἕτοιμος, -η, -ον, *ready, prepared*

θησαυρός, -οῦ, ὁ, *a storehouse, treasure* (*thesaurus*)

ἵππος, -ου, ὁ, *a horse* (*hippo*potamus, literally, a river-horse)

καθάπερ, *even as, as*

καταλύω, *I destroy; I lodge* (cf. *catalyze*)

κερδαίνω, *I gain*

νίπτω, *I wash*

νυμφίος, -ου, ὁ, *a bridegroom* (akin to *nuptial*)

περιτέμνω, *I circumcize*

πλήρωμα, -ατος, τό, *fullness* (*pleroma*, in Valentinian Gnosticism, the world of light, including the body of eons)

πλησίον, *near*; as a noun, *a neighbor*

πολλάκις, *often*

ποταμός, -οῦ, ὁ, *a river* (hippo*potamus*, literally, a river-horse)

ῥύομαι, *I rescue, deliver*

σκοτία, -ας, ἡ, *darkness* (*scoto*scope, a field-glass for seeing by night)

χάρισμα, -ατος, τό, *a gift* (freely and graciously given) (*charism*, a special spiritual gift or power divinely conferred; 1 Cor. 12)

ὡσαύτως, *likewise*


WORDS OCCURRING 16 TIMES

ἀθετέω, *I reject* (*athetize*, to reject a text or passage as spurious)

ἀνακρίνω, *I examine*

ἀπάγω, *I lead away*

δεῖπνον, -ου, τό, *a supper*

δηνάριον, -ου, τό, *a denarius* (*denarius*)

διαλογίζομαι, *I debate*

διατάσσω, *I command*

διψάω, *I thirst* (cf. *dipso*mania, a craving for alcohol)

ἐκτείνω, I stretch forth (cf. extend)
ἐκχέω, I pour out
ἐντέλλομαι, I command
ἔπειτα, then
ἐπιθυμέω, I desire
ἐργάτης, -ου, ὁ, a workman (cf. energy)
εὐλογία, -ας, ἡ, a blessing (eulogy)
ζῆλος, -ου, ὁ, zeal, jealousy (zeal)
θεμέλιος, -ου, ὁ, a foundation
κακῶς, badly
κατέρχομαι, I come down, go down
κλείω, I shut
κλέπτης, -ου, ὁ, a thief (kleptomaniac)
οὐδέποτε, never
πάθημα, -ατος, τό, suffering (cf. pathological; apathy)
παρέχω, I offer, afford
πέτρα, -ας, ἡ, a rock (petrify)
πλήρης, -ες, full
προσδοκάω, I wait for
ῥαββί, indeclinable, ὁ, (my) master (rabbi)
ῥίζα, -ης, ἡ, a root (cf. rhizome)
συκῆ, -ῆς, ἡ, a fig tree (sycophant, a flatterer, literally, a fig-shower [the
    reason for the name is not definitely known])
συλλαμβάνω, I take, conceive
συνίστημι or συνιστάνω, transitive tenses, I commend; intransitive
    tenses, I stand with, consist
σφραγίς, -ῖδος, ἡ, a seal (sphragistics, the science of seals, their history,
    age, distinctions, etc.)
τέρας, -ατος, τό, a wonder
τολμάω, I dare
τροφή, -ῆς, ἡ, food (cf. atrophy, wasting due to malnutrition)
ὑστερέω, I lack
χορτάζω, I eat to the full, am satisfied, am filled
ὦ, O!


WORDS OCCURRING 15 TIMES

ἀνέχομαι, I endure
γεύομαι, I taste (cf. gusto, disgust)

30

γνωστός, -ή, -όν, known
γυμνός, -ή, -όν, naked (gymnasium)
δέρω, I beat
διαμαρτύρομαι, I testify solemnly
ἐλαία, -ας, ἡ, an olive tree
ἐπαγγέλλομαι, I promise
εὐσέβεια, -ας, ἡ, piety, godliness (Eusebius)
εὐχαριστία, -ας, ἡ, thanksgiving (Eucharist)
θρίξ, τριχός, ἡ, a hair (trichina, a thread-like worm)
καταλαμβάνω, I overtake, apprehend
κατεσθίω, I eat up, devour
κλάω, I break (iconoclast, literally, a breaker of images)
κληρονόμος, -ου, ὁ, an heir
κτίζω, I create
λῃστής, -οῦ, ὁ, a robber
λύπη, -ης, ἡ, pain, grief
μοιχεύω, I commit adultery
νήπιος, -ου, ὁ, an infant, child
νομίζω, I suppose
ξηραίνω, I dry up (cf. xerophagy, among early Christians, the practice
    of living on a diet of dry food, especially during Lent and other
    fasts)
ὅθεν, whence, wherefore
οἰκουμένη, -ης, ἡ, the (inhabited) world (cf. ecumenical)
ὁμοιόω, I make like, liken (homoeoteleuton, the occurrence of the same
    or similar endings of lines, a frequent source of error in copied
    manuscripts)
παρθένος, -ου, ἡ, a virgin (parthenogenesis)
παύομαι, I cease
ποτίζω, I give drink to (akin to potion)
σαλεύω, I shake
σκάνδαλον, -ου, τό, a cause of stumbling (scandal)
συμφέρω, I bring together; impersonally, it is profitable
σφραγίζω, I seal (cf. sphragistics, the science of seals, their history, age,
    distinctions, etc.)
τράπεζα, -ης, ἡ, a table (trapeze, so called from the square or rectangle
    formed by the ropes and crossbar)
τύπος, -ου, ὁ, mark, example (type)
ὑπακοή, -ῆς, ἡ, obedience

31

χόρτος, -ου, ὁ, *grass, hay*
ὠφελέω, *I profit*

WORDS OCCURRING 14 TIMES

ἄκανθαι, -ῶν, αἱ, *thorns* (the *acanthus* plant)
ἀλλότριος, -α, -ον, *another's, strange*
ἀμφότεροι, -αι, -α, *both*
ἀνάκειμαι, *I recline* (at meals)
ἀναχωρέω, *I depart*
ἀνθίστημι, *I resist*
ἀνομία, -ας, ἡ, *lawlessness*
ἅπαξ, *once, once for all*
ἀπειθέω, *I disbelieve, disobey*
ἀτενίζω, *I look intently, gaze upon intently*
αὔριον, *tomorrow*
ἀφίστημι, *I withdraw, depart*
γράμμα, -ατος, τό, *a letter* (of the alphabet); plural, *writings*
διαλογισμός, -οῦ, ὁ, *a reasoning, questioning* (cf. *dialogue*)
ἕκτος, -η, -ον, *sixth*
ἐλάχιστος, -η, -ον, *least*
ἐνιαυτός, -οῦ, ὁ, *a year*
ἐπίσταμαι, *I understand* (cf. *epistemology*, the science of the methods and grounds of knowledge)
εὐφραίνω, *I rejoice* (cf. *Euphrosyne*, one of the three Graces in Greek mythology)
κατανοέω, *I observe*
κληρονομία, -ας, ἡ, *an inheritance*
κοινός, -ή, -όν, *common, unclean* (ceremonially)
κοινόω, *I make common, I defile* (ceremonially) (cf. *cenobite*, one dwelling in a convent community [where all is held in common])
κωφός, -ή, -όν, *deaf, dumb*
λύχνος, -ου, ὁ, *a lamp*
μακρόθεν, *from afar, afar*
μακροθυμία, -ας, ἡ, *long-suffering, patience, forbearance*
μερίζω, *I divide*
μέτρον, -ου, τό, *a measure* (*meter*)
μύρον, -ου, τό, *ointment*
μωρός, -ά, -όν, *foolish* (*moron*)

32

νοέω, I understand (noetic)

ξένος, -η, -ον, strange; as a noun, a stranger, host (the chemical element xenon)

οἷος, -α, -ον, such as

ὄφις, -εως, ὁ, a serpent (Ophites, Gnostics who revered the serpent as the symbol of hidden, divine wisdom)

ὀψία, -ας, ἡ, evening

πετεινά, -ῶν, τά, birds

προσδέχομαι, I receive, wait for

σεισμός, -οῦ, ὁ, an earthquake (seismograph)

σῖτος, -ου, ὁ, wheat (parasite, literally, one who sits by [παρά] another's food and eats at his expense)

στηρίζω, I establish

τάλαντον, -ου, τό, a talent (talent)

ταπεινόω, I humble

φρόνιμος, -η, -ον, prudent

χωλός, -ή, -όν, lame


WORDS OCCURRING 13 TIMES

ἀνά, with the acc., upwards, up; with numerals, each; ἀνὰ μέσον, into the midst, among

ἀναγγέλλω, I announce, report

ἀναλαμβάνω, I take up

ἀναστροφή, -ῆς, ἡ, conduct

ἄνωθεν, from above, again

ἁρπάζω, I seize (cf. harpoon, harpy)

βοάω, I cry aloud

βουλή, -ῆς, ἡ, counsel, purpose

δαιμονίζομαι, I am demon possessed (demonize)

διαλέγομαι, I dispute (dialectics)

διαφέρω, I differ

δράκων, -οντος, ὁ, a dragon (dragon)

εἶτα, then

ἐκπλήσσομαι, I am astonished, amazed

ἐλεημοσύνη, -ης, ἡ, alms (eleemosynary; alms)

ἐμπαίζω, I mock

ἕξ, six (Hexapla, the edition of the Old Testament compiled by Origen, in the third century, comprising six columns)

33

ἐξαποστέλλω, *I send forth*
ἔξωθεν, with the gen., *from without*
ἐπιζητέω, *I seek for*
ἐπιπίπτω, *I fall upon*
ζύμη, -ης, ἡ, *leaven* (enzyme)
θερισμός, -οῦ, ὁ, *harvest* (cf. *thermal*)
θύω, *I sacrifice, kill* (*thyme*)
καπνός, -οῦ, ὁ, *smoke*
καταισχύνω, *I put to shame*
κατακαίω, *I burn up*
καταντάω, *I come to*
καταρτίζω, *I mend, fit, perfect*
κλέπτω, *I steal* (cf. *clept*omania)
παιδεύω, *I teach, chastise* (cf. *ped*agogue)
παιδίσκη, -ης, ἡ, *a maid servant*
παράδοσις, -εως, ἡ, *a tradition*
πρίν, *before*
πώς, *at all, somehow, in any way*
συνεργός, -οῦ, ὁ, *a fellow worker* (cf. *synergism*, the semi-Pelagian doctrine that there are two efficient agents in regeneration, namely the human will and the divine Spirit, which, in the strict sense of the term, co-operate)
τίμιος, -α, -ον, *precious, honorable*, (cf. *Timothy*, honoring God)
τρόπος, -ου, ὁ, *manner, way* (in rhetoric, *trope*, a figurative use of a word)
τύπτω, *I smite* (cf. *tympanum*, the middle ear)
ὕψιστος, -η, -ον, *highest*
φύσις, -εως, ἡ, *nature* (*physics*)
χρυσίον, -ου, τό, *gold* (cf. *chrys*anthemum, literally, golden flower)
χωρίζω, *I separate, depart*


WORDS OCCURRING 12 TIMES

ἄδικος, -ον, *unjust*
ἀλέκτωρ, -ορος, ὁ, *a cock* (cf. *alectry*omancy, divination by means of a cock encircled by grains of corn placed on letters of the alphabet, the letters being then put together in the order in which the grains were eaten)
ἀναπαύω, *I refresh*; middle: *I take rest*
ἀναπίπτω, *I recline*

34

ἀπαρνέομαι, I deny

ἀσκός, -οῦ, ὁ, a (leather) bottle, wine-skin (in botany, ascidium, the leaf of the pitcher plant)

αὐλή, -ῆς, ἡ, a court (in Austro-German history, the Aulic Council)

βαπτιστής, -οῦ, ὁ, baptist (Baptist)

βασανίζω, I torment

βῆμα, -ατος, τό, judgment seat (in ecclesiastical architecture, bema, the inner part of the chancel, reserved for the clergy)

βροντή, -ῆς, ἡ, thunder (brontosaurus, literally, thunder-lizard)

γέεννα, -ης, ἡ, gehenna (Gehenna)

γόνυ, -ατος, τό, a knee (akin to genuflect)

δεῦτε, come!

διάνοια, -ας, ἡ, the mind, understanding, a thought

δίκτυον, -ου, τό, a net

ἔθος, -ους, τό, a custom (ethics)

ἐξάγω, I lead out

ἐξουθενέω, I despise

ἔσωθεν, from within, within

καίω, I burn (caustic)

κἀκεῖ (= καὶ ἐκεῖ), and there

κάλαμος, -ου, ὁ, a reed (calamus)

κατάκειμαι, I lie down, lie sick, recline (at meals)

κολλάομαι, I join, cleave to (cf. colloid)

κομίζω, I receive

κράτος, -ους, τό, power, dominion (cf. democracy, rule of the people)

λίαν, greatly

λιμός, -οῦ, ὁ, hunger, famine (in medicine, limosis, excessive and morbid hunger)

λυχνία, -ας, ἡ, a lampstand

μάλιστα, especially

ὀδούς, -όντος, ὁ, a tooth (odontology)

οἰκοδεσπότης, -ου, ὁ, a householder

ὅραμα, -ατος, τό, a vision (panorama, a complete [πᾶν] view)

ὅρια, -ων, τά, boundaries (cf. horizon)

παραιτέομαι, I make excuse, refuse

πιάζω, I take

πληθύνω, I multiply

πλουτέω, I am rich (cf. plutocrat)

πόρνη, -ης, ἡ, a prostitute (pornography)

35

πρόθεσις, -εως, ἡ, a setting forth; a purpose (in the Eastern Church, the prothesis, referring to the placing of the eucharistic elements)
προσλαμβάνω, I receive
πρωΐ, in the morning, early
πῶλος, -ου, ὁ, a colt
ῥάβδος, -ου, ἡ, a staff, rod (rhabdomancy, divination by rods)
σαλπίζω, I sound a trumpet
σπλαγχνίζομαι, I have compassion (splanchnic)
σπουδή, -ῆς, ἡ, haste, diligence
στήκω, I stand, stand fast
συνέχω, I hold fast, oppress
ταχύ, quickly (tachygraphy, stenography, especially that of the ancient Greeks and Romans)
τρίς, thrice (in liturgics, the Trisagion)
τυγχάνω, I obtain, happen
ὑγιαίνω, I am in good health (cf. hygiene)
ὑγιής, -ές, whole, healthy (cf. hygiene)
ὑψηλός, -ή, -όν, high
φιάλη, -ης, ἡ, a cup, bowl (phial, vial)
φονεύω, I kill, murder
χοῖρος, -ου, ὁ, a pig
ψεύδομαι, I lie (pseudo-)


WORDS OCCURRING 11 TIMES

ἀγαλλιάω, I exult
ἀγορά, -ᾶς, ἡ, a market-place (agora)
ἅλυσις, -εως, ἡ, a chain
ἀναστρέφω, I return; I live
ἀπιστία, -ας, ἡ, unbelief
ἀρχαῖος, -α, -ον, old, ancient (archaic)
ἄφρων, -ον, foolish
βρῶσις, -εως, ἡ, eating, food, rust
γέμω, I fill
δάκρυ, -υος, and δάκρυον, -ου, τό, a tear (akin to lachrymal)
διαμερίζω, I divide, distribute
δόλος, -ου, ὁ, guile
δωρεά, -ᾶς, ἡ, a gift
ἐάω, I permit

εἴδωλον, -ου, τό, an image, idol (idol)
εἴκοσι, twenty (icosahedron, a geometric figure with twenty faces)
εἰσάγω, Ι lead in
ἐκχύννομαι, Ι pour out
ἔλαιον, -ου, τό, olive-oil (akin to oil, oleo-)
ἐλευθερία, -ας, ἡ, liberty
ἐμβλέπω, Ι look at
ἐνδείκνυμαι, Ι show forth
ἔπαινος, -ου, ὁ, praise
ἐπαισχύνομαι, Ι am ashamed
ἐπισκέπτομαι, Ι visit, have a care for (cf. episcopal)
ζηλόω, Ι am zealous (cf. zeal)
ζωοποιέω, Ι make alive
θανατόω, Ι put to death (cf. thanatopsis)
θάπτω, Ι bury (cf. cenotaph; epitaph)
κακία, -ας, ἡ, malice, evil
καταβολή, -ῆς, ἡ, a foundation (cf. katabolism)
κατασκευάζω, Ι prepare
κάτω, down, below
καύχημα, -ατος, τό, a boasting, ground of boasting
καύχησις, -εως, ἡ, boasting
κέρας, -ατος, τό, horn (rhinoceros, literally, nose-horn)
κλάδος, -ου, ὁ, a branch (of a tree) (in botany, cladophyll)
κλῆρος, -ου, ὁ, a lot (that which is cast or drawn); a portion (clergy; cleric, clerk)
κλῆσις, -εως, ἡ, a (divine) call, invitation, summons
κλητός, -ή, -όν, called
κράβαττος, -ου, ὁ, a mattress, pallet, bed (of a poor man)
λίμνη, -ης, ἡ, a lake (limnology, the scientific study of ponds and lakes)
μεταβαίνω, Ι depart
νεανίσκος, -ου, ὁ, a youth
νόσος, -ου, ἡ, a disease (nosophobia, a morbid fear of disease)
ὁμοθυμαδόν, with one accord
ὀνειδίζω, Ι reproach
παράγω, Ι pass by
παραλυτικός, -οῦ, ὁ, a paralytic (paralytic)
παρεμβολή, -ῆς, ἡ, a camp, army, fortress
περισσοτέρως, more abundantly
πηγή, -ῆς, ἡ, a spring, fountain

37

ποιμαίνω, I shepherd, rule (poimenic, pertaining to pastoral theology)
πρᾶγμα, -ατος, τό, a deed, matter, thing (pragmatic)
πραΰτης, -ῆτος, ἡ, gentleness, humility, courtesy
πρότερος, -α, -ον, former; as an adverb, before (cf. proto-)
πυνθάνομαι, I inquire
σάλπιγξ, -ιγγος, ἡ, a trumpet
σπλάγχνα, -ων, τά, bowels; heart, tender mercies, compassion (splanchnic)
σπουδάζω, I hasten, am eager
σφόδρα, exceedingly
σχίζω, I split (schism; schizophrenia)
τελευτάω, I die
τριάκοντα, indeclinable, thirty
ὑμέτερος, -α, -ον, your
ὑπαντάω, I meet, go to meet
ὑποκάτω, under, below, down at
ὕστερον, later, afterwards (in rhetoric, hysteron-proteron, a reversing of
   the natural order of the sense, as 'he is well and lives')
φυτεύω, I plant
φωτίζω, I give light, enlighten (cf. photo-)
χείρων, -ον, worse, more severe
χίλιοι, -αι, -α, a thousand (chiliasm, millenarianism)
χιτών, -ῶνος, ὁ, a tunic (chiton)
χράομαι, I use (catachresis, misuse of a word; in rhetoric, a mixed
   metaphor)
χρυσός, -οῦ, ὁ, gold (chrysanthemum)
ψευδοπροφήτης, -ου, ὁ, a false prophet


WORDS OCCURRING 10 TIMES

ἁγιασμός, -οῦ, ὁ, sanctification
ᾅδης, -ου, ὁ, Hades (Hades)
ἀδύνατος, -ον, incapable, impossible
ἀκαθαρσία, -ας, ἡ, uncleanness
ἅμα, at the same time; with the dat., together with
ἀνατολή, -ῆς, ἡ, east, dawn (Anatolia)
ἀναφέρω, I bring up, offer
ἄνομος, -ον, lawless, without law
ἀπολογέομαι, I defend myself (cf. apology)
ἀπολύτρωσις, -εως, ἡ, redemption

38

ἀσέλγεια, -ας, ἡ, licentiousness, debauchery, sensuality
ἀσπασμός, -οῦ, ὁ, a greeting
ἀφαιρέω, I take away (aphaeresis, dropping of a letter or syllable from the
    beginning of a word, as 'lone' from 'alone')
ἀφορίζω, I separate (aphorism)
βίβλος, -ου, ἡ, a book (Bible)
βίος, -ου, ὁ, life (biology)
δεσπότης, -ου, ὁ, a master, lord (despot)
διατρίβω, I continue (diatribe, a prolonged and acrimonious harangue)
δικαίωμα, -ατος, τό, regulation, righteous deed
διωγμός, -οῦ, ὁ, persecution
ἐγκαταλείπω, I leave behind, forsake, abandon
ἐκκόπτω, I cut out, cut off
ἐκπίπτω, I fall away
ἐμφανίζω, I manifest
ἔνατος, -η, -ον, ninth (Ennead, one division of the collection made by
    Porphyry of the teachings of Plotinus, arranged in six divisions of
    nine books each)
ἔνοχος, -ον, involved in, liable, guilty
ἐξομολογέομαι, I confess, profess (in the ancient Church, exomologesis, the
    public confession of sin, usually accompanied by fasting, weeping,
    and mourning)
ἐπειδή, since, because
ἐπιδίδωμι, I give to
ἐπιτάσσω, I command
ἐπιτελέω, I complete, perform
θλίβω, I press, oppress
ἰσχύς, -ύος, ἡ, strength
κἀκεῖθεν (= καὶ ἐκεῖθεν), and from there; and then
κοινωνός, -οῦ, ὁ, a partner, sharer (cf. cenobite, one dwelling in a convent
    community)
κοσμέω, I adorn (cosmetics)
μακράν, far away
μακροθυμέω, I am patient
μέλει, it is a care
μνῆμα, -ατος, τό, grave, tomb
νομικός, -ή, -όν, pertaining to the law; as a noun, one skilled in the Mosaic
    law, a lawyer
ξενίζω, I entertain (a stranger); I startle, bewilder

ὅδε, ἥδε, τόδε, *this* (here)

οἰκονόμος, -ου, ὁ, *a steward* (economy)

ὀνομάζω, *I name* (cf. onomasticon, a collection of proper names)

ὄντως, *really* (cf. ontology)

ὅρκος, -ου, ὁ, *an oath*

παντοκράτωρ, -ορος, ὁ, *ruler of all, the Almighty*

πατάσσω, *I smite*

πενθέω, *I mourn*

περιστερά, -ᾶς, ἡ, *a dove*

πλάνη, -ης, ἡ, *a wandering, error* (cf. *planet*, which to the ancients was apparently a *wandering* celestial body)

πλατεῖα, -ας, ἡ, *a street* (place)

πλεονεξία, -ας, ἡ, *covetousness*

ποικίλος, -η, -ον, *varied, manifold*

πόρνος, -ου, ὁ, *a fornicator* (pornography)

προέρχομαι, *I go in front, precede*

προσκαρτερέω, *I continue in* or *with*

πύλη, -ης, ἡ, *a gate, porch* (pylon)

σέβομαι, *I reverence, worship*

σιγάω, *I am silent, become silent*

σιωπάω, *I am silent* (apo*siopesis*, in rhetoric, a figure of speech in which the speaker breaks off suddenly)

στρατηγός, -οῦ, ὁ, *a commander*

συγγενής, -ές, *kindred*; as a noun, *a relative, kinsman*

συζητέω, *I discuss, dispute*

σύνδουλος, -ου, ὁ, *a fellow slave*

σφάζω, *I slay*

τάσσω, *I arrange, appoint, order* (cf. *tactics*)

ταχέως, *quickly* (cf. *tachy*graphy)

τέταρτος, -η, -ον, *fourth* (cf. *tetrarch*, a ruler over a fourth part)

ὑπόδημα, -ατος, τό, *a sandal, shoe*

φείδομαι, *I spare*

χρηστότης, -ητος, ἡ, *goodness, kindness*

χωρίον, -ου, τό, *a place, field* (cf. *choro*graphy, describing, or description, of districts)

ψεῦδος, -ους, τό, *a lie* (cf. *pseudo-*)

ψεύστης, -ου, ὁ, *a liar* (cf. *pseudo-*)

# PART II

# WORDS CLASSIFIED ACCORDING TO THEIR ROOT

AFTER the student has mastered about four or five hundred words of frequent occurrence in the Greek Testament, he can begin to use with profit the following groups of words arranged according to their root. Here are collected those words, scattered throughout Part I, which are related to each other by reason of a common etymology. Each group was formed in accord with the requirement that it must contain at least three words each of which occurs ten or more times in the New Testament. In addition to the words from Part I that satisfy this arbitrary requirement, there have been added about 250 other words, each of which occurs from five to nine times in the New Testament. It will be discovered that these words of comparatively infrequent occurrence can be learned with very little additional effort when they are thus grouped with others derived from the same root.

## THE FORMATION OF WORDS

Words do not grow haphazardly or in isolation from the rest of the vocabulary. To see how verbs, nouns, adjectives, adverbs, and particles can be traced to a relatively few basic roots is not only a fascinating study in itself, but it also lessens the drudgery of piecemeal memorization of individual words. Thus, for example, from the root *TEΛ*, meaning *end*, is formed the noun τέλος with the same meaning. From the noun a verb is produced, τελέω, meaning *I finish* or *fulfill* (that is, *I make an appropriate end*). From the noun comes also the adjective τέλειος, meaning *complete, perfect, mature* (that is, *brought to its appropriate end*). The adjective, again, is made into the verb τελειόω, which means *I complete, make perfect*—being equivalent to τέλειον ποιέω. Moreover, the same root *TEΛ* appears in τελευτάω, a verb formed ultimately from τέλος and which means *I die* (that is, *I come to the end [of my life]*). Finally, to complete the list of all the words from this root which appear in the New Testament five times or more, by composition with prepositions the compound words ἐπιτελέω, συντέλεια, and συντελέω are formed, each of which involves some aspect of the root idea of *end*.

This example illustrates the principle of the building of Greek words. The root is the primitive part of the word; it conveys the basic meaning or idea. From the root are produced various verb-stems and noun-stems (the latter of which produce both nouns and adjectives). These stems are built (1) by the addition of various suffixes and/or (2) by the internal modification of the stem. The following is a simplified classification of some of the more important ways in which the words of the Greek Testament are formed. For a more complete technical description, any large reference grammar of New Testament Greek should be consulted.[1]

The suffix is a formative element standing between the root and the declensional or conjugational ending. Suffixes limit or particularize the basic meaning of the root. Some suffixes[2] have special meanings, and when these are known it is often possible to deduce the general significance of an unfamiliar Greek word by analyzing the root idea in the stem as qualified by the suffix.

## A. Suffixes forming nouns

The following suffixes are listed with the ending of the nominative case, singular number, attached. The numeral within the parentheses following the suffix indicates the declension of the nouns formed with that suffix.

1. The *agent* is indicated by -της (1).

Examples: βαπτισ-τής (from βαπτίζω), *one who baptizes, a baptizer, baptist*

μαθη-τής (from μανθάνω), *one who learns, a learner, disciple*

2. An *action* is indicated by -μος (2) and -σις (3). The latter suffix often produces the abstract name of an action.

---

[1] The best treatment is that by J. H. Moulton and W. F. Howard, *A Grammar of New Testament Greek*, vol. ii, *Accidence and Word-Formation* (Edinburgh, 1929), pp. 268–410.

[2] It should be noted that roots, stems, and suffixes never existed as independent words in Greek, or indeed in any known period of the parent language from which Greek and the other Indo-European tongues were derived. The analysis of words into their component morphological elements is merely a scientific device useful for purposes of arrangement and classification.

Examples: βαπτισ-μός (from βαπτίζω), a washing, purification (the act of which βάπτισμα is the result; see below)
καθαρισ-μός (from καθαρίζω), a cleansing, purification
ἀπολύτρω-σις (from ἀπολυτρόω, I release on payment of a ransom), a releasing effected by payment of a ransom (λύτρον), redemption
δικαίω-σις (from δικαιόω), an act of adjudging one to be righteous, justification

3. The result of an action is indicated by -μα (3).

Examples: βάπτισ-μα (from βαπτίζω), baptism (the abiding fact resulting from the act of baptism; see above, βαπτισμός)
γράμ-μα (from γράφω), thing written, a letter (of the alphabet)
κήρυγ-μα (from κηρύσσω), thing proclaimed by a herald, preaching

4. The abstract idea of quality is indicated by -ια (1), -οτης (3), and -συνη (1).

Examples: σοφ-ία, wisdom
σωτηρ-ία, salvation
κυρι-ότης, lordship, dominion
νε-ότης, youth
ἀγαθω-σύνη, goodness
δικαιο-σύνη, righteousness

B. Suffixes forming adjectives

1. Adjectivēs expressing the meaning of or belonging to a person or thing are formed by adding the suffix -ιος to a noun-stem.

Examples: οὐράν-ιος, heavenly (from οὐρανός, heaven)
πλούσ-ιος, wealthy (from πλοῦτος, wealth)
τίμ-ιος, precious, honorable (from τιμή, honor, price)

2. Adjectives expressing the idea belonging to, pertaining to, with the characteristics of, are formed by adding the suffix -ικος to a noun-stem.

Examples: βασιλ-ικός, belonging to a king, kingly, royal (from βασιλεύς, a king)
πνευματ-ικός, pertaining to the spirit, with the characteristics of the spirit, spiritual (from πνεῦμα, spirit)
σαρκ-ικός, fleshly, carnal (from σάρξ, flesh)
σωματ-ικός, pertaining to the body, bodily (from σῶμα, body)

43

3. Adjectives which express the *material* from which anything is made are formed with the suffix -ινος.

Examples: δερμάτ-ινος, *of skin, leathern*
δίθ-ινος, *of stone*
σάρκ-ινος, *of the flesh*

4. Many other adjectival suffixes have no characteristic signification. Some of these are -ος, -λος, -νος, -ανος, -μος, and -ρος.

5. A special class of adjectives, called verbal adjectives, is formed by the suffix -τος. These either (*a*) have the meaning of a perfect passive participle or (*b*) express *possibility*.

Examples: (*a*) ἀγαπη-τός, *beloved*
εὐλογη-τός, *blessed*
κρυπ-τός, *hidden*
(*b*) ἀνεκ-τός, *bearable, tolerable*

In general the passive sense is more common. Some have either signification, as ἀδύνα-τος, *incapable* or *impossible*.

*C. Suffixes forming verbs*

From the original verb-stem, which is ordinarily preserved unchanged in the second aorist stem, the present stem is formed in various ways, some of which are the following. It will be observed that not only are suffixes employed but also an internal modification of the stem may take place (called *Ablaut*).

1. The verb-stem may remain unchanged.

Examples: ἄγ-ω, *I lead*
δέ-ω, *I bind*
λύ-ω, *I loose*

2. The initial consonant of the verb-stem may undergo reduplication.

Examples: γίνομαι, *I become,* from the stem γεν- (classical γίγνομαι, from *γι-γέν-ομαι)[1]
δί-δω-μι, *I give,* from the stem δο-
ἵ-στη-μι *I cause to stand,* from the stem στα- (for *σί-στη-μι)
πίπτω, *I fall,* from the stem πετ- (for *πι-πέτ-ω)

[1] An asterisk preceding a Greek word here and in the list below signifies that the word, though preserved in no extant source, must be postulated as the parent of existing forms.

44

3. The vowel in the verb-stem may be lengthened.

Examples: λείπ-ω, *I leave*, from λιπ- (cf. 2nd aor. ἔ-λιπ-ον)
πείθ-ω, *I persuade*, from πιθ- (cf. 2nd aor. ἔ-πιθ-ον)
φεύγ-ω, *I flee*, from φυγ- (cf. 2nd aor. ἔ-φυγ-ον)

4. The final consonant of the verb-stem may be doubled.

Examples: ἀπο-στέλλ-ω, *I send away*, from στελ-
βάλλ-ω, *I throw*, from βαλ- (cf. 2nd aor. ἔ-βαλ-ον)

5. Another consonant may be added to the verb-stem, as -ν-, -σκ-, or -τ-.

Examples: θνή-σκω, *I die*, from θαν- (cf. 2nd aor. ἔ-θαν-ον)
πί-νω, *I drink*, from πι- (cf. 2nd aor. ἔ-πι-ον)
τύπ-τω, *I strike*, from τυπ- (cf. 2nd aor. ἔ-τυπ-ον)

6. An additional syllable may be added to the verb-stem.

(*a*) The ending -άνω, sometimes with ν (μ before a labial) inserted in the verb-stem, may be added.

Examples: ἁμαρτ-άνω, *I sin*, from ἁμαρτ- (cf. 2nd aor. ἥμαρτ-ον)
μανθ-άνω, *I learn*, from μαθ- (cf. 2nd aor. ἔ-μαθ-ον)

(*b*) The endings -άζω, -ίζω, or -ύζω may be added.

Examples: λιθ-άζω, *I stone*
ἐλπ-ίζω, *I hope*
γογγ-ύζω, *I grumble, murmur*

(*c*) The endings -άω, -έω, or -εύω may be added. These usually denote an action or state similar to that expressed by the noun-stem.

Examples: ἀγαπ-άω, *I love*, from ἀγάπη, *love*
δουλ-εύω, *I serve* (*as a slave*), from δοῦλος, *a slave*
φιλ-έω, *I love, am friendly towards*, from φίλος, *a friend*

(*d*) The endings -αίνω, -όω, or -ύνω may be added. These usually express causation, except in verbs of mental action such as ἀξι-όω, *I deem worthy*, δικαι-όω, *I deem* or *judge* or *pronounce righteous*.

Examples: δουλ-όω, *I enslave*, from δοῦλος, *a slave*
πικρ-αίνω, *I make bitter, embitter*, from πικρός, *sharp, bitter*
πληθ-ύνω, (transitive) *I multiply*, (intransitive) *I abound*, from πλῆθος, *a multitude*

45

(*e*) Some Greek verbs are 'irregular,' that is, their present stem is entirely different from their aorist stem (and frequently other stems likewise). Thus, φέρω means *I carry*, but ἤνεγκα means *I carried*; ἐσθίω means *I eat*, ἔφαγον means *I ate*. The reason for the existence of these irregular verbs is simply that the aorist tense of one verb and the present tense of another verb of quite similar meaning both fell into disuse. The remaining present and aorist tenses of these two verbs then came to be associated together as though they were related etymologically. The same thing has happened in languages other than Greek. In English the verb *went* is not the etymological preterit of *go*; it is the past tense of the little-used verb *wend*. Further, modern English rejects the earlier preterit of *go* (the Anglo-Saxon *eode* and Middle English *yode*). The tenses that remain of each verb now function as the principal parts of one verb. In French, to take an example of irregularity within the same tense, the first and second persons plural of the present tense of the verb *aller*, 'to go,' are *nous allons, vous allez*, but the other forms of the present tense are *je vais, tu vas*, etc. The conjugation of the verb is irregular because behind the different forms lie two different Latin words which, for some reason, came to be preferred in those persons (they are *ambulare* and *vadare*, both meaning 'to walk, go').[1]

The irregular verbs which (with their compounds) occur most frequently in the Greek New Testament are the following. A hyphen before a principal part means that this form appears only in compound verbs.

αἱρέω, *I take*, middle, *I choose*, fut. αἱρήσομαι and -ελῶ, 2nd aor. -εἷλον, middle εἱλάμην, perf. -ῄρημαι, aor. passive -ῃρέθην.

εἷπον and εἷπα, *I said*, fut. ἐρῶ, perf. εἴρηκα, perf. passive εἴρημαι, aor. passive ἐρρέθην and ἐρρήθην.

ἔρχομαι, *I come, go*, fut. ἐλεύσομαι, 2nd aor. ἦλθον, perf. ἐλήλυθα.

ἐσθίω and ἔσθω, *I eat*, fut. φάγομαι, 2nd aor. ἔφαγον.

ὁράω, *I see*, fut. ὄψομαι, 2nd aor. εἷδον, perf. ἑώρακα and ἑόρακα, aor. passive ὤφθην.

τρέχω, *I run*, 2nd aor. ἔδραμον.

φέρω, *I carry*, fut. οἴσω, aor. ἤνεγκα and -ἤνεγκον, perf. -ἐνήνοχα, aor. passive ἠνέχθην.

---

[1] The Italian verb *andare* exhibits the same irregularity: *noi andiamo, voi andate*, but *io vado, tu vai*, etc.

46

Everything set forth above refers to the building of simple words from one stem. Compound words, on the other hand, are formed from a union of two or more stems or parts, as ψευδο-προφήτης, *a false prophet*, and ἀντι-παρ-ῆλθεν, *he passed by* [παρά] *on the other side* [ἀντί], used of the priest and the Levite in the parable of the Good Samaritan (Luke 10: 31 f.). As can be observed from these two examples, a compound word contains a defining part and a defined part, usually in this order.

The parts of a compound word stand in various syntactical relations to each other, as that of adjective or attributive genitive to a noun, or that of adverb or object to a verb, etc. Compounds may thus be regarded as abbreviated forms of syntax. In analyzing the meaning of a compound, it must be kept in mind that no part of the word is without significance.

Compound words are formed chiefly in the following three ways.

1. Various particles and adverbs may be prefixed. The two of most frequent occurrence are:

(*a*) The alpha privative, ἀ- (before vowels generally ἀν-), which gives a negative sense to the word to which it is affixed (cf. the English prefix 'un-').

Examples: ἄ-δικος, *unjust*
ἀ-τιμάζω, *I dishonor*
ἀν-έγκλητος, *unreprovable, blameless*

(*b*) The adverbial prefix εὐ-, which supplies the general idea of 'prosperously,' 'being well disposed.'

Examples: εὐ-δοκέω, *I am well pleased, think it good*
εὐ-λογέω, *I speak well of, praise, bless*

2. One or more prepositions may be prefixed. For detailed information concerning this very large class of compound verbs, see Appendix II.

3. Two or more noun-stems or verb-stems may be compounded. As regards their meaning, compound nouns (substantives and adjectives) may be divided into two principal classes.

(*a*) Objective compounds. In these the first part is related to the other as a kind of grammatical object. When the two are expressed

47

in English as separate words, the first is put in an oblique case depending, either immediately or by means of a preposition, on the other.

Examples: θεό-πνευστος, *inspired by God*
νομο-διδάσκαλος, *a teacher of* [*the*] *Law*
οἰκο-δεσπότης, *a master of a house, a householder*

(*b*) Possessive and descriptive compounds. In these the first part qualifies the second as an adjective or adverb.

Examples: μακρο-θυμία, *long-suffering*
μον-όφθαλμος, *one-eyed, having one eye*
ὀλιγό-πιστος, *having little faith*
ταπεινο-φροσύνη, *lowliness of mind, humility*

In drawing up the following ninety-six groups of words the author has tried to avoid two extremes. He has tried to refrain from spinning out fanciful derivations for the sake of establishing connections between words which, according to scientific linguistics, are entirely unrelated. No statement about root or derivation is made which involves a descent to the level of popular or folk-etymology. If a root is obscure or uncertain—or even merely probable—it has not been given.[1] The other extreme which he has tried to avoid is the cumbering of the lists with technical details of advanced linguistics. It may very well be, for example, that originally there was but one root ΛΕΓ which meant 'gather, pick' as well as 'say,' but it is not inaccurate to differentiate between the two by forming two separate lists of words involving each of these meanings; and certainly such an arrangement is less liable to engender confusion than the other.

Finally, it ought to be mentioned that several of the roots contain the obsolete Greek letter *vau*, ϝ, called 'digamma' (i.e. *double-gamma*) from its shape.[2] The sound of this letter was like that of English *w*. Thus, the root ϜΙΔ, 'see,' lies behind εἶδον (for ε-ϝιδ-ον) and the second perfect tense οἶδα, *I know* (literally, *I have seen*) ; compare other Indo-

[1] The chief authorities upon which the etymologies are based are Walther Prellwitz, *Etymologisches Wörterbuch der griechischen Sprache*, 2nd edn. (Göttingen, 1905), and Émile Boisacq, *Dictionnaire étymologique de la langue grecque*, 3rd edn. (Heidelberg and Paris, 1938).
[2] *Vau* had not entirely disappeared in pronunciation when the Homeric epics were composed, and not a few apparent irregularities of meter in these poems can be explained by postulating its influence. For a discussion of the letter, see Edgar H. Sturtevant, *The Pronunciation of Greek and Latin*, 2nd edn. (Philadelphia, 1940), pp. 65–8, and W. Sidney Allen, *Vox Graeca* (Cambridge, 1968), pp. 45–50.

European words, such as Sanskrit *ved-a*, 'knowledge'; Latin *vid-eo*, 'I see'; German *wis-sen*, 'know'; Anglo-Saxon *wit-an* (English *to wit* and the archaic *wot* [means 'know'; see Acts 3:17, Rom. 11:2, etc., in the King James Version]).

root ΑΓ, 'drive, lead, weigh'

ἄγω, *I lead*
ἀνάγω, *I lead up*; middle, *I put to sea, set sail*
ἀπάγω, *I lead away*
εἰσάγω, *I lead in, bring in*
ἐξάγω, *I lead out*
παράγω, *I pass by*
περιάγω, *I lead about, go about*
προάγω, *I lead forth, go before*
συνάγω, *I gather together*
συναγωγή, -ῆς, *a synagogue*
ἀρχισυνάγωγος, -ου, ὁ, *a ruler of a synagogue*
ἐπισυνάγω, *I collect, gather together at one place*
ὑπάγω, *I depart*
ἀγρός, -οῦ, ὁ, (place where cattle are *led* or *driven*), *a field*
ἡγέομαι, *I am chief*; (*I lead through the mind*), *I think, regard*
ἡγεμών, -όνος, ὁ, *a leader, governor*
ἄξιος, -α, -ον, (*of equal weight*), *worthy*
ἀξιόω, *I deem worthy, think fit*
ἀξίως, *worthily*
ἀγών, -ῶνος, ὁ, *an athletic contest, a contest*

root ΑΓ, 'religious awe, reverence'

ἅγιος, -α, -ον, *holy*
ἁγιάζω, *I make holy, sanctify*
ἁγιασμός, -οῦ, ὁ, *sanctification*
ἁγνός, -ή, -όν, (in a condition prepared for worship), *pure* (ethically, ritually, or ceremonially), *chaste*
ἁγνίζω, *I make pure*

49

ἀγαπάω, I love
ἀγάπη, -ης, ἡ, love
ἀγαπητός, -ή, -όν, beloved

---

ἄγγελος, -ου, ὁ, a messenger, an angel
ἀναγγέλλω, I announce, report
ἀπαγγέλλω, I announce, report
ἐπαγγελία, -ας, ἡ, a promise
ἐπαγγέλλομαι, I promise
εὐαγγελίζω, I bring good news, preach good tidings (the Gospel)
εὐαγγέλιον, -ου, τό, good news, the Gospel
καταγγέλλω, I proclaim
παραγγέλλω, I command, charge
παραγγελία, -ας, ἡ, a command

---

αἰτέω, I ask
αἰτία, -ας, ἡ, a cause, accusation
παραιτέομαι, I make excuse, refuse

---

ἀκούω, I hear
εἰσακούω, I hearken to, assent to
ὑπακούω, I obey
ἀκοή, -ῆς, ἡ, hearing, a report
ὑπακοή, -ῆς, ἡ, obedience

## root ΑΛΛ, 'other'

ἄλλος, -η, -ο, other, another
ἀλλήλων, (reduplicated stem, αλλ-ηλο), of one another
ἀλλά, (neuter plural with changed accent: 'in another way'), but
ἀλλάσσω, (I make other than it is), I change, alter
καταλλάσσω, I change (from enmity to friendship), reconcile

## root ΑΡ, 'join, fit'

ἀρέσκω, (I fit or join together; suit), I please
ἀριθμός, -οῦ, ὁ, a number
ἄρτι, (fitting exactly), now, just now
ἀρετή, -ῆς, ἡ, (moral fitness), virtue, excellence

50

# root ΑΡΧ, 'be first'

ἄρχω, (first in point of station), I rule; middle, (first in point of time), I begin
ἄρχων, -οντος, ὁ, a ruler
ἀρχή, -ῆς, ἡ, a beginning
ἀρχαῖος, -α, -ον, old, ancient
ἀρχιερεύς, -έως, ὁ, a chief priest, high priest
ὑπάρχω, (I am under as a foundation, support), I am, I exist, I belong to (τὰ ὑπάρχοντα, one's belongings, possessions)
ἀπαρχή, -ῆς, ἡ, first fruits

# root ΒΑ, 'go'

ἀναβαίνω, I go up
ἐμβαίνω, (I step into [a boat]), I embark
ἐπιβαίνω, I go up to, mount, board (a boat)
καταβαίνω, I go down
μεταβαίνω, I depart
παράβασις, -εως, ἡ, (a going over [the line]), transgression, a transgression
παραβάτης, -ου, ὁ, a transgressor
προβαίνω, I go forward, go on
πρόβατον, -ου, τό, a sheep (that which goes forward)
συμβαίνω, (of events) happen, occur
βῆμα, -ατος, τό, judgment seat (that which the judge mounts)
βέβαιος, -α, -ον, (reduplicated stem, βε-βα-, standing fast), solid, sure, firm
βεβαιόω, I confirm, ratify
βέβηλος, -η, -ον, (lawful to be trodden), profane, secular

# root ΒΑΛ, 'throw'

βάλλω, I throw, put
ἐκβάλλω, I cast out
ἐπιβάλλω, I lay upon
λιθοβολέω, I pelt with stones, kill by stoning
περιβάλλω, I put around, clothe
συμβάλλω, (I throw together), I encounter, meet, consider; middle, contribute to
ὑπερβάλλω, (I surpass in throwing), I surpass, exceed
διάβολος, -ου, ὁ, (one who throws across or at, with words, a slanderer), the accuser, the Devil
καταβολή, -ῆς, -ἡ, (that which is put down), a foundation

51

παραβολή, -ῆς, ἡ (a placing of one thing by the side of another, by way of comparison), a parable
παρεμβολή, -ῆς, ἡ, a camp, army, fortress
ὑπερβολή, -ῆς, ἡ, (a throwing beyond), excess, abundance

---

βασιλεύς, -έως, ὁ, a king
βασιλεύω, I reign
βασιλεία, -ας, ἡ, a kingdom
βασιλικός, -ή, -όν, kingly, royal

## root ΒΑΦ, 'dip'

βαπτίζω, I baptize
βάπτισμα, -ατος, τό, baptism
βαπτιστής, -οῦ, ὁ, baptizer, Baptist (used only of John)

---

βλέπω, I see
ἀναβλέπω, I look up, receive sight
ἐμβλέπω, I look at
περιβλέπομαι, I look around, survey

## root ΓΕΝ, 'beget, become'

γίνομαι, (Attic, γίγνομαι, a reduplicated form, = *γι-γέν-ομαι), I become, come into being, happen, am made, am
παραγίνομαι, I come, arrive
γονεύς, -έως, ὁ, a parent
γένος, -ους, τό, race, kind
μονογενής, -ές, only, unique, only-begotten
συγγενής, -ές, related; a relative, kinsman
γενεά, -ᾶς, ἡ, a generation
γένεσις, -εως, ἡ, birth, origin
γένημα, -ατος, τό, fruit, produce
γεννάω, I beget

## root ΓΝΟ, 'know'

γινώσκω, I know
ἀναγινώσκω, (I know again), I read

ἐπιγινώσκω, I come to know, recognize
γνῶσις, -εως, ἡ, wisdom
ἐπίγνωσις, -εως, ἡ, knowledge
προγινώσκω, I know beforehand, foreknow
γνωρίζω, I make known
γνωστός, -ή, -όν, known; as a noun, an acquaintance
γνώμη, -ης, ἡ, opinion, counsel
ἀγνοέω, I do not know

root *ΓΡΑΦ*, 'scratch, scrape' (signs in stone or wood)
γράφω, I write
γραφή, -ῆς, ἡ, a writing, Scripture
ἐπιγράφω, I write upon, inscribe
ἐπιγραφή, -ῆς, ἡ, an inscription
γράμμα, -ατος, τό, a letter (of the alphabet), writing
γραμματεύς, -έως, ὁ, a scribe

root *ΔΕ*, 'bind'
δέω, I bind
δέσμιος, -ου, ὁ, a prisoner
δεσμός, -οῦ, ὁ, a fetter, bond
ὑπόδημα, -ατος, τό (that which is bound under [the foot]), a sandal, shoe

root *ΔΕΙΚ*, 'show, point'
δείκνυμι and δεικνύω, I show
ἐνδείκνυμαι, I show
ἐπιδείκνυμι, I show, prove
ὑποδείκνυμι, I show, indicate, warn
ὑπόδειγμα, -ατος, τό, an example, copy

root *ΔΕΚ*, 'take'
δέχομαι, I take, receive
ἀποδέχομαι, I accept from, receive, welcome
ἐκδέχομαι, I expect, wait for
ἀπεκδέχομαι, I wait for eagerly
παραδέχομαι, I accept, receive
προσδέχομαι, I receive, wait for
εὐπρόσδεκτος, -ον, well-received, acceptable

53

προσδοκάω, *I wait for*
δεξιός, -ά, -όν, [δεκ+σ = δεξ], *right* (perhaps because the *right* hand
is oftenest used in *taking*)

---

διάκονος, -ου, ὁ and ἡ, *a servant, deacon, deaconess*
διακονέω, *I serve, wait upon, care for one's needs, minister*
διακονία, -ας, ἡ, *the office and work of a διάκονος, service, ministry*

---

διδάσκω, *I teach*
διδάσκαλος, -ου, ὁ, *a teacher*
διδασκαλία, -ας, ἡ, *teaching*
διδαχή, -ῆς, ἡ, *teaching*

### root ΔΙΚ, 'show, point'

δίκαιος, -α, -ον, *righteous* (in accord with the way *pointed* out)
δικαιόω, *I justify, pronounce righteous*
δικαιοσύνη, -ης, ἡ, *righteousness*
δικαίωμα, -ατος, τό, *regulation, righteous deed*
δικαίως, *justly, uprightly*
ἐκδικέω, *I avenge*
ἀδικέω, *I wrong, do wrong*
ἄδικος, -ον, *unjust*
ἀδικία, -ας, ἡ, *unrighteousness*
ἀντίδικος, -ου, ὁ, *an opponent in a suit at law, an adversary*
ἐκδίκησις, -εως, ἡ, *vengeance, punishment*

### root ΔΟ, 'give'

δίδωμι, *I give*
ἀποδίδωμι, *I give back, pay*; middle, *I sell*
ἀνταποδίδωμι, *I give back (in return)*
ἐπιδίδωμι, *I give to*
μεταδίδωμι, *I share with, impart*
παραδίδωμι, *I hand over, betray*
παράδοσις, -εως, ἡ, *a tradition (that which has been handed over)*
δωρεά, -ᾶς, ἡ, *a gift*
δωρεάν, (accusative of the noun, used adverbially: *as a gift, gift-wise*),
  *freely*
δῶρον, -ου, τό, *a gift*

## root *ΔOK*, 'beseem, befit'

δοκέω, *I think; I seem*
εὐδοκέω, *I think it good, am well pleased with*
εὐδοκία, -ας, ἡ, *good will, favor, pleasure, approval*
συνευδοκέω, *I entirely approve of, agree with*
δόξα, -ης, ἡ, *glory*
δοξάζω, *I glorify*
δοκιμάζω, *I prove, approve*
ἀποδοκιμάζω, *I reject (after testing)*
δοκιμή, -ῆς, ἡ, *a proving, approval, character*
δόκιμος, -ον, *tested, approved*
ἀδόκιμος, -ον *(failing to pass the test), unapproved, counterfeit*
δόγμα, -ατος, τό, *a (public) decree*

---

δοῦλος, -ου, ὁ, *a slave*
σύνδουλος, -ου, ὁ, *a fellow slave*
δουλεία, -ας, ἡ, *slavery*
δουλεύω, *I serve*
δουλόω, *I enslave*

---

δύναμαι, *I am powerful, able*
ἐνδυναμόω, *I endue with power, make strong*
δύνατος, -η, -ον, *powerful, possible*
ἀδύνατος, -ον, *impossible*
δύναμις, -εως, ἡ, *power*

---

ἔλεος, -ους, τό, *pity, mercy*
ἐλεέω, *I have mercy*
ἐλεημοσύνη, -ης, ἡ, *alms*

## root *'EPX*, 'come, go'

ἔρχομαι, *I come, go*
ἀπέρχομαι, *I depart*
διέρχομαι, *I pass through*
εἰσέρχομαι, *I go in*
ἐξέρχομαι, *I go out*
ἐπέρχομαι, *I come upon* (sometimes with hostility)
κατέρχομαι, *I come down, go down*

55

παρέρχομαι, *I pass by, pass away*
προέρχομαι, *I go before*
προσέρχομαι, *I come to*
συνέρχομαι, *I come together*

## root 'ΕΣ, 'be'

εἰμί, *I am*
ἄπειμι, *I am absent*
πάρειμι, *I am present; I have arrived*
παρουσία, -ας, ἡ, *presence, coming* (especially Christ's [second] coming in glory)
ἔξεστι, *it is permitted, it is lawful*
ἐξουσία, -ας, ἡ, *authority*

## root 'ΕΧ and ΣΕΧ, 'have'

ἔχω, *I have, hold*
ἀνέχομαι, (*I bear up*), *I endure*
ἀνεκτός, -όν, *bearable, tolerable*
ἀπέχω, *I have received* (payment); *I am distant*
ἐπέχω, *I hold out, give attention to*
κατέχω, *I hold fast, hold back*
μετέχω, *I have a share in, partake of*
μέτοχος, -ον, *sharing in*; as a noun, *a partner*
παρέχω, *I offer, afford*
προσέχω, *I attend to, give heed to*
συνέχω, (*I hold together, constrain*), *I hold fast, oppress*
ὑπερέχω, (*I hold over, above*), *I rise above, am superior*
ἔνοχος, -ον, ( = ἐνερχόμενος, *held in, bound by*), *liable, guilty*
εὐσχήμων, -ον, *of elegant figure* (way of *holding* oneself), *grace, of good standing*
μετασχηματίζω, *I change the figure of, transfigure*

## root FEP, 'speak'

ἐρῶ, (from a rare present stem, εἴρω), *I shall say*
ῥῆμα, -ατος, τό, *a word*
παρρησία, -ας, ἡ, *boldness* (of speech), *confidence*
παρρησιάζομαι, *I speak boldly*

root ϜΕΡΓ, 'work'

ἔργον, -ου, τό, work
ἐργάτης, -ου, ὁ, a workman
ἐνεργέω, I work, effect
συνεργέω, I work along with, co-operate with
συνεργός, -οῦ, ὁ and ἡ, a fellow worker
ἐργάζομαι, I work
ἐργασία, -ας, ἡ, work, business, profit
κατεργάζομαι, I work out
γεωργός, -οῦ, ὁ, (a worker in the earth [γῆ]), a farmer
λειτουργός, -οῦ, ὁ, (a public [λαός] minister), a servant
πανουργία, -ας, ἡ, (ability to do anything, cleverness), craftiness, cunning
ἀργός, -όν, idle, lazy (contracted from ἀ-εργός)
καταργέω, I bring to naught, abolish

root ϜΙΔ, 'see'

εἶδον, I saw
εἶδος, -ους, τό, visible form, shape
εἴδωλον, -ου, τό, an image, idol
εἰδωλολάτρης, -ου, ὁ, an idolater
οἶδα, (second perfect [I have seen] with present sense), I know
ᾅδης, -ου, ὁ, (a privative and ϝιδ, the unseen world), Hades

ζάω, I live
ζωή, -ῆς, ἡ, life
ζῷον, -ου, τό, a living creature, an animal

ζητέω, I seek
ἐκζητέω, I seek out
ἐπιζητέω, I seek for
συνζητέω, I question with, discuss
ζήτημα, -ατος, τό, a question, debate
ζήτησις, -εως, ἡ, a questioning, debate

root ΘΑΝ, 'die'

θνήσκω, I die; perfect tense, I am dead
θνητός, -ή, -όν, liable to death, mortal

57

ἀποθνήσκω, I die
θάνατος, -ου, ὁ, death
θανατόω, I put to death

## root ΘΕ, 'put, set, place'

τίθημι, I place
ἀποτίθεμαι, I put off from myself, lay aside
διατίθημι, I appoint, make a covenant
ἐπιτίθημι, I lay upon
μετατίθημι, I transfer, change
παρατίθημι, I set before; middle, I entrust
περιτίθημι, I place around, clothe
προστίθημι, I add, I add to
ἀθετέω, I reject
θεμέλιος, -ου, ὁ, a foundation
θεμελιόω, I lay the foundation of, establish
ἀποθήκη, -ης, ἡ, a storehouse, granary, barn
διαθήκη, -ης, ἡ, a covenant
ἀνάθεμα, -ατος, τό, (a thing laid by or set up; a thing devoted to the
  vengeance of God), a curse, a man accursed

## root ΘΥ (1), 'burn, smoke'

θύω, I sacrifice, kill
θυμίαμα, -ατος, τό, incense
θυσία, -ας, ἡ, a sacrifice
θυσιαστήριον, -ου, τό, (a place for sacrifice), an altar

## root ΘΥ (2), 'rush'

θυμός, -οῦ, ὁ, wrath
ἐπιθυμέω, (I have it upon my heart), I desire
ἐπιθυμία, -ας, ἡ, eager desire, passion
μακροθυμέω, I am patient
μακροθυμία, -ας, ἡ, long-suffering
ὁμοθυμαδόν, with one accord
προθυμία, -ας, ἡ, eagerness, enthusiasm

58

# root Ἱ, 'set in motion'

ἄνεσις, -εως, ἡ, a loosening; relief, rest
ἀφίημι, I let go, permit, forgive
ἄφεσις, -εως, ἡ, a sending away, remission
συνίημι, (I go along with), I understand
σύνεσις, -εως, ἡ, understanding
ἀσύνετος, -ον, without understanding, stupid

---

ἰσχύς, -ύος, ἡ, strength
ἰσχυρός, -ά, -όν, strong
ἰσχύω, I am strong

# root ΚΑΘ, 'clean'

καθαρός, -ά, -όν, clean
καθαρίζω, I cleanse
καθαρισμός, -οῦ, ὁ, a cleansing, purification
ἀκαθαρσία, -ας, ἡ, uncleanness
ἀκάθαρτος, -ον, unclean

# root ΚΑΛ, 'call'

καλέω, I call
κλητός, -ή, -όν, called
κλῆσις, -εως, ἡ, a (divine) call, invitation
ἐγκαλέω, I call to account, accuse
ἀνέγκλητος, -ον, not to be called to account, unreprovable, blameless
ἐκκλησία, -ας, ἡ, a church, the Church
ἐπικαλέομαι, I call, name; middle, I invoke, appeal to
παρακαλέω, (I call beside myself), I beseech, exhort, console
παράκλησις, -εως, ἡ, exhortation, consolation
παράκλητος, -ου, ὁ, an intercessor, helper, Paraclete
προσκαλέομαι, I summon
συνκαλέω, I call together, assemble

---

καυχάομαι, I boast
καύχημα, -ατος, τό, a boasting, a ground of boasting
καύχησις, -εως, ἡ, boasting

## root *KEI*, 'lie outstretched'

κεῖμαι, *I lie*
ἀνάκειμαι, *I recline* (at meals)
ἀντίκειμαι, *I resist, oppose*
ἐπίκειμαι, *I lie upon, press upon, am urgent*
κατάκειμαι, *I lie down, lie sick*; *I recline* (at meals)
περίκειμαι, *I am compassed about with, have around me*
πρόκειμαι, *I am set before, am present*
συνανάκειμαι, *I recline together, feast together*
κοιμάομαι, (*I lie at rest*), *I sleep, fall asleep, die*
κώμη, -ης, ἡ, *a village*

---

κλῆρος, -ου, ὁ, *a lot, a portion*
κληρονόμος, -ου, ὁ, *an heir*
κληρονομέω, *I inherit*
κληρονομία, -ης, ἡ, *an inheritance*

---

κοινός, -ή, -όν, *common, unclean*
κοινόω, *I make common, defile*
κοινωνέω, *I have a share of, take part in*
κοινωνία, -ας, ἡ, *fellowship, collection*
κοινωνός, -οῦ, ὁ and ἡ, *a partner, sharer*

## root *KOΠ*, 'cut, strike'

κόπτω, *I cut*; middle, *I strike* (my breast or head in lamentation)
ἀποκόπτω, *I cut off, amputate*
ἐκκόπτω, *I cut out, cut off*
ἐνκόπτω, (*I cut into*), *I block, hinder*
προσκόπτω, *I strike against, stumble, stumble at*
πρόσκομμα, -ατος, τό, *a stumbling, a stumbling-block, an obstacle*
κόπος, -ου, ὁ, *trouble, labor*
εὔκοπος, -ον, *with easy labor, easy*
κοπιάω, *I toil*

## root *KPAT* and *KAPT*, 'strong, hard'

κράτος, -ους, τό, *power, dominion*
κρατέω, *I grasp*
κρείσσων, (or κρείττων), -ονος, *better*

60

προσκαρτερέω, *I continue in* or *with*
παντοκράτωρ, -ορος, ὁ, *ruler of all, the Almighty*

### root ΚΡΙ, 'separate'

κρίνω, *I judge, decide*
ἀνακρίνω, *I examine*
ἀποκρίνομαι, *I answer*
διακρίνω, *I discriminate*; middle, *I doubt*
κατακρίνω, *I condemn*
κρίμα, -ατος, τό, *judgment*
κρίσις, -εως, ἡ, *judgment*
κριτής, -οῦ, ὁ, *a judge*
ὑποκριτής, -οῦ, ὁ, *a hypocrite* (literally, *a pretender, an actor*)
ὑπόκρισις, -εως, ἡ, (*acting a part*), *hypocrisy*
ἀνυπόκριτος, -ον, *unfeigned, undisguised*

### root ΛΑΒ, 'take, receive'

λαμβάνω, *I take, receive* (2nd aor. ἔ-λαβ-ον)
ἀναλαμβάνω, *I take up*
ἐπιλαμβάνω, *I take hold of*
καταλαμβάνω, *I undertake, apprehend*
μεταλαμβάνω, *I have a share of, partake of, get*
παραλαμβάνω, *I receive*
προσλαμβάνω, *I receive*
συλλαμβάνω, *I take, conceive*
ὑπολαμβάνω, *I take up* (by supporting beneath); *I welcome*; *I catch up*
  (in speech); *I suppose*

### root ΛΑΘ, 'conceal'

λανθάνω, *I am hidden from, escape notice* (2nd aor. ἔ-λαθ-ον)
ἐπιλανθάνομαι, *I forget, neglect*
ἀληθής, -ές, *true* (not concealed)
ἀληθινός, -ή, -όν, *true*
ἀλήθεια, -ας, ἡ, *truth*
ἀληθῶς, *truly*

### root ΛΕΓ (1), 'gather, pick'

διαλέγομαι, (*I pick out* [thoughts] *one from another*), *I dispute*
διάλεκτος, -ου, ἡ, *speech, language*
ἐκλέγομαι, *I pick out, choose*

ἐκλεκτός, -ή, -όν, chosen, elect
ἐκλογή, -ῆς, ἡ, a choosing out, election (in the New Testament always of the *divine choice*)

## root ΛΕΓ (2), 'say'

λέγω, I say, speak
λόγος, -ου, ὁ, a word, the Word
εὐλογέω, (*I speak well of someone*), I bless
εὐλογητός, -όν, blessed
εὐλογία, -ας, ἡ, a blessing
ἀπολογέομαι, I defend myself
ἀπολογία, -ας, ἡ, a defense (especially in a law court)
λογίζομαι, I account, reckon
διαλογίζομαι, I debate
διαλογισμός, -οῦ, ὁ, a reasoning, questioning

## root ΛΥ, 'loose'

λύω, I loose
ἀπολύω, I release (*loose from*)
ἀπολύτρωσις, -εως, ἡ, (*a releasing*), redemption
ἐκλύομαι, I am unstrung, grow weary, become faint-hearted
καταλύω, (*I dissolve*), I destroy; I lodge (after having *loosed* the straps and packs of the beasts of burden as well as one's own garments)
παραλύομαι, (*I am unstrung*), I am a paralytic
παραλυτικός, -ή, -όν, paralytic

## root ΜΑ, 'reflex thought, persistency'

μένω, (*I bethink myself, wait*), I remain
διαμένω, I remain throughout
ἐπιμένω, I remain in
προσμένω, I remain with, continue in
ὑπομένω, I tarry; I endure
ὑπομονή, -ῆς, ἡ, patient, steadfast endurance
μιμητής, -οῦ, ὁ, an imitator
μιμνήσκομαι, I remember
ἀναμιμνήσκομαι, I call to remembrance
ὑπομιμνήσκω, I bring to remembrance
μνεία, -ας, ἡ, remembrance, mention

62

μνῆμα, -ατος, τό, (something that brings to remembrance), *a sepulcher, tomb, monument*
μνημεῖον, -ου, τό, *a sepulcher, tomb, monument*
μνημονεύω, *I remember*


## root *MAP*, 'thoughtful'

μάρτυς, -υρος, ὁ and ἡ, *a witness*
μαρτυρέω, *I bear witness, testify*
μαρτυρία, -ας, ἡ, *testimony, evidence*
μαρτύριον, -ου, τό, *a testimony, witness, proof*
διαμαρτύρομαι, *I testify (solemnly)*


## root *MEP*, 'part'

μέρος, -ους, τό, *a part*
μερίζω, *I divide* (make parts of)
διαμερίζω, *I divide, distribute*


## root *NEM*, 'allot'

νόμος, -ου, ὁ, *a law, the Law*
ἀνομία, -ας, ἡ, *(without law), lawlessness*
νομίζω, *I suppose, think*
νομικός, -ή, -όν, *relating to law*; as a noun, *one learned in the (Mosaic) law, a lawyer*


## root *NO*, 'know'

νοέω, *I understand*
νόημα, -ατος, τό, *a thought, a design*
διάνοια, -ας, ἡ, *the mind, understanding, a thought*
κατανοέω, *I observe*
μετανοέω, *I repent*
μετάνοια, -ας, ἡ, *repentance*
νοῦς, νοός, ὁ, *the mind*
νουθετέω, *(I put in mind), I admonish, warn, exhort*

---

63

οἶκος, -ου, ὁ, *a house*
οἰκοδεσπότης, -ου, ὁ, *a householder*
οἰκοδομέω, *I build, edify*
οἰκοδομή, -ῆς, ἡ, *a building; edification*
ἐποικοδομέω, *I build upon, build up*
οἰκονόμος, -ου, ὁ, *a steward*
οἰκέω, *I dwell, inhabit*
ἐνοικέω, *I dwell in*
κατοικέω, *I inhabit, dwell*
οἰκονομία, -ας, ἡ, *stewardship, arrangement, dispensation*
οἰκουμένη, -ης, ἡ, *the (inhabited) world*
οἰκία, -ας, ἡ, *a house*

root ʼOM, 'like'

ὅμοιος, -α, -ον, *like*
ὁμοιόω, *I make like, liken*
ὁμοίωμα, -ατος, τό, *a likeness, image*
ὁμολογέω, (*I say the same thing*), *I confess, profess*
ἐξομολογέομαι, *I confess, profess*
ὁμολογία, -ας, ἡ, *a confession, profession*

root ʼOΠ, 'see'

ὄψομαι, (ὄπ-σο-μαι), *I shall see*
ὀφθαλμός, -οῦ, ὁ, *an eye*
μέτωπον, -ου, τό, *forehead*
πρόσωπον, -ου, τό, *face*

---

πάσχω, *I suffer* (2nd aor. ἔ-παθ-ον)
πάθημα, -ατος, τό, *suffering*
πενθέω, *I mourn*

---

παῖς, παιδός, ὁ and ἡ, *a boy, girl, child, servant*
παιδεύω, *I teach, chastise*
παιδεία, -ας, ἡ, *discipline, chastisement*
παιδίον, -ου, τό, *an infant, child*
παιδίσκη, -ης, ἡ, *a maid-servant*
ἐμπαίζω, *I mock*

πᾶς, πᾶσα, πᾶν, *every, all*
ἅπας, -ασα, -αν, (used by some authors in preference to πᾶς after a consonant), *all*
πανταχοῦ, *everywhere*
πάντως, *entirely, assuredly*
παντοκράτωρ, -ορος, ὁ, *ruler of all, the Almighty*

### root ΠΕΡ (1), 'press or drive through'

πορεύομαι, *I go, proceed*
διαπορεύομαι, *I go through*
εἰσπορεύομαι, *I enter*
ἐκπορεύομαι, *I go out*
παραπορεύομαι, *I go past, pass by*
ἔμπορος, -ου, ὁ, (*one on a journey* [especially for business]), *a merchant*
πέραν, *beyond* (*on the further side*)
διαπεράω, *I cross over*
ἀπορέω, (*I lose the way*), *I am in doubt, perplexed*

### root ΠΕΡ (2), causal of ΠΕΡ (1), 'export for sale'

πιπράσκω, (for reduplicated πι-περ-ασκω), *I sell*
πορνεύω, *I commit fornication*; metaphorically of idolatry (in accord with Biblical imagery, the marriage relationshp between God and his people is broken by the worship of idols)
πορνεία, -ας, ἡ, *fornication*
πόρνη, -ης, ἡ, (*one whose body is sold*), *a prostitute, harlot*
πόρνος, -ου, ὁ, *a fornicator*

### root ΠΕΤ, 'fly, fall'

πέτομαι, *I fly*
πετεινά, -ῶν, τά, *birds*
καταπέτασμα, -ατος, τό, *a veil* (spread out), *a curtain*
πίπτω, (for reduplicated πι-πετ-ω), *I fall*
ἀναπίπτω, *I recline*
ἐκπίπτω, *I fall away*
ἐμπίπτω, *I fall into*
ἐπιπίπτω, *I fall upon*
προσπίπτω, *I fall towards, prostrate myself before*

65

πτέρυξ, -υγος, ἡ, a wing
πτῶμα, -ατος, τό, (the fallen body of one dead), a corpse
παράπτωμα, -ατος, τό, (a fall beside), a sin, trespass

## root ΠΙ and ΠΟ, 'drink'

πίνω, I drink
καταπίνω, I drink down, devour, swallow up
ποτήριον, -ου, τό, a cup
ποτίζω, I give drink to

## root ΠΙΘ, 'bind'

πείθω, I persuade (hind myself)
ἀπειθέω, I disbeliive, disobey (not let myself be bound)
ἀπείθεια, -ας, ἡ, disobedience, rebellion
ἀπειθής, -ές, disobedient
πεποίθησις, -εως, ἡ, trust, confidence
πίστις, -εως, ἡ, faith, belief, trust
πιστός, -ή, -όν, faithful, believing
ἄπιστος, -ον, unbelieving, faithless
ἀπιστία, -ας, ἡ, unbelief
ὀλιγόπιστος, -ον, of little faith
πιστεύω, I have faith (in), believe
ἀπιστέω, I am unfaithful, disbelieve

## root ΠΛΑ, 'fill'

πίμπλημι, I fill
ἐμπίπλημι and ἐμπιπλάω, I fill up
πλήρης, -ες, full
πληρόω, I fill, fulfill
ἀναπληρόω, I fill up
πλήρωμα, -ατος, τό, fullness
πλῆθος, -ους, τό, a multitude
πληθύνω, I multiply
πολύς, πολλή, πολύ, much; plural, many
πλείων, -ον, larger, more

66

πλεονάζω, I abound in, make to abound
πλεονεκτέω, (I have more), I gain the advantage of, defraud
πλεονεξία, -ας, ἡ, greedy desire to have more, covetousness

### root ΣΑϜ, 'safe and sound, alive and well'

σώζω, I save
διασώζω, I save (rescue) though (some danger)
σωτήρ, -ῆρος, ὁ, a savior, rescuer, preserver, the Saviour
σωτηρία, -ας, ἡ, salvation
σωφρονέω, I am sober-minded, self-controlled

---

(σθένος, -ους, τό, strength, might [not in the New Testament])
ἀσθενής, -ες, weak
ἀσθενέω, I am weak
ἀσθένεια, -ας, ἡ, lack of strength, weakness, illness

### root ΣΚΑ, 'cover, darken'

σκηνή, -ῆς, ἡ, a tent, tabernacle
σκηνόω, I dwell in a tent, encamp
σκιά, -ᾶς, ἡ, a shadow
ἐπισκιάζω, I overshadow, envelop
σκότος, -ους, τό, darkness
σκοτία, -ας, ἡ, darkness
σκοτίζομαι, I am covered with darkness, darkened

### root ΣΤΑ, 'stand, set'

ἵστημι, I cause to stand; I stand
ἀνθίστημι, (I stand against), I resist
ἀνίστημι, I cause to rise; I arise
ἀφίστημι, I withdraw, depart
ἐνίστημι, I am at hand, am present
ἐξίστημι, (I set one out of his senses), I amaze, am amazed
ἐφίστημι, I stand over, come upon
ἐπιστάτης, -ου, ὁ, (one standing over another), a master (found only in
    Luke, used of Jesus)
ἐπίσταμαι, I understand, know
καθίστημι, I set, constitute
ἀποκαθίστημι and ἀποκαθιστάνω, I set up again, restore to its former state

67

μεθίστημι and μεθιστάνω, *I transfer, remove*
παρίστημι, *I am present, stand by*
προΐστημι, *I stand in front, lead, rule, practice*
συνίστημι and συνιστάνω, *I recommend; I stand with, consist*
στάσις, -εως, ἡ, *a standing; an insurrection*
ἀνάστασις, -εως, ἡ, (*a standing up*), *resurrection*
ἔκστασις, -εως, ἡ, (*standing outside oneself*), *bewilderment, a trance*
ὑπόστασις, -εως, ἡ, (*a standing under*), *substance, confidence*
ἀκαταστασία, -ας, ἡ, *instability, disturbance, revolution*

<h2 style="text-align:center">root ΣΤΑΥ or ΣΤΑϜ, lengthened form of ΣΤΑ</h2>

σταυρός, -οῦ, ὁ, *a cross*
σταυρόω, *I crucify*
συνσταυρόω, *I crucify along with*

<h2 style="text-align:center">root ΣΤΕΛ, 'set in order, equip'</h2>

ἀποστέλλω, *I send away* (with a commission)
ἀπόστολος, -ου, ὁ, *an Apostle*
διαστέλλομαι, *I command, charge expressly*
ἐξαποστέλλω, *I send forth*
ἐπιστολή, -ῆς, ἡ, (*thing sent by a messenger*), *a letter*
στολή, -ῆς, ἡ, (*a piece of equipment*, especially of clothes, *apparel*), *a long robe, a festal robe*

<h2 style="text-align:center">root ΣΤΡΕΦ, 'turn'</h2>

στρέφω, *I turn*
ἀναστρέφω, *I return; I behave, live*
ἀναστροφή, -ῆς, ἡ, *conduct*
διαστρέφω, *I pervert*
ἐπιστρέφω, *I turn to, return*
ὑποστρέφω, *I return*

<h2 style="text-align:center">root ΤΑΓ, 'arrange, order'</h2>

τάσσω, *I arrange, appoint, order*
ἀντιτάσσομαι, *I range in battle against, resist*
ἀποτάσσομαι, *I separate myself, take leave of, forsake*
διατάσσω, *I command*
ἐπιτάσσω, *I command*
ἐπιταγή, -ῆς, ἡ, *a command, order, authority*

ὑποτάσσω, *I subject*
τάξις, -εως, ἡ, *an arrangement, order, right order, office*

## root *ΤΕΛ*, 'end'

τέλος, -ους, τό, *end*
τελέω, *I finish, fulfill*
ἐπιτελέω, *I complete, perform*
συντελέω, *I finish, accomplish*
συντέλεια, -ας, ἡ, *completion, consummation*
τέλειος, -α, -ον, *complete, perfect, mature*
τελειόω, *I complete, make perfect*
τελευτάω, (*I come to the end of life*), *I die*

---

τέσσαρες, -αρα, *four*
δεκατέσσαρες, -αρα, *fourteen*
τεσσαράκοντα, indeclinable, *forty*
τέταρτος, -η, -ον, *fourth*
τράπεζα, -ης, ἡ, (*four-footed*), *a table*

## root *ΤΙ*, 'honor, pay'

τιμή, -ῆς, ἡ, *honor, price*
τιμάω, *I honor*
ἐπιτιμάω, *I rebuke, warn*
τίμιος, -α, -ον, *honorable, precious*
ἀτιμάζω, *I dishonor, insult*
ἀτιμία, -ας, ἡ, *dishonor, disgrace*
ἔντιμος, -ον, *held in honor, precious, prized*

---

τρεῖς, τρία, *three*
τριάκοντα, indeclinable, *thirty*
τρίτος, -η, -ον, *third*
τρίς, *thrice, three times*

---

ὑψηλός, -ή, -όν, *high*
ὕψιστος, -η, -ον, *highest*
ὕψος, -ους, τό, *height, heaven*
ὑψόω, *I lift up, exalt*

root *ΦΑϜ*, *ΦΑ*, and *ΦΑΝ*, 'shine, show'

φαίνω, *I shine, appear*
ἐπιφάνεια, -ας, ἡ, *an appearing, manifestation* (of Christ in glory)
ἀφανίζω, (*I make unseen*), *I destroy*; passive, *I vanish*
ἐμφανίζω, *I manifest*
φανερός, -ά, -όν, *manifest*
φανερόω, *I make manifest*
ὑπερήφανος, -ον, (*showing onself above others*), *haughty, disdainful*
φημί, (*I bring to light, make known*), *I say*
προφητεύω, *I prophesy*
προφητεία, -ας, ἡ, *a prophecy*
προφήτης, -ου, ὁ, *a prophet*
φωνή, -ῆς, ἡ, *a sound, voice*
φωνέω, *I call*
συμφωνέω, *I am in accord, agree with*
βλασφημέω, *I blaspheme*
βλασφημία, -ας, ἡ, *blasphemy*
πρόφασις, -εως, ἡ, *a pretense, pretext*
φῶς, (contracted from φάος), φωτός, τό, *light*
φωτεινός, -ή, -όν, *shining, brilliant*
φωτίζω, *I shed light on, enlighten*

root *ΦΕΡ*, 'bear'

φέρω, *I carry, bear, lead*
ἀποφέρω, *I carry off, bear away*
διαφέρω, (*I bear apart*), *I differ*
εἰσφέρω, *I bring in, into*
ἐκφέρω, *I carry out, bring out*
προσφέρω, *I bring to, offer*
προσφορά, -ᾶς, ἡ, *an offering, a sacrifice*
συμφέρω, *I bring together*; *it is profitable*
φορέω, *I bear, carry, wear*
καρποφορέω, *I bear fruit*
πληροφορέω, *I accomplish, satisfy fully, fully convince*
φορτίον, -ου, τό, *a burden, load*

root *ΦΡΕΝ* (in φρήν, *midriff, heart, mind*)

φρονέω, *I think*
καταφρονέω, *I despise, scorn*

70

σωφρονέω, *I am sober-minded, self-controlled*
ταπεινοφροσύνη, -ης, ἡ, *lowliness of mind, humility*
φρόνιμος, -η, -ον, *prudent*
ἄφρων, -ον, *foolish*
εὐφραίνω, *I gladden, cheer up*; *am glad, rejoice*

root *ΦΥ*, 'bring forth'

φυλή, -ῆς, ἡ, *a tribe*
φύλλον, -ου, τό, *a leaf*
φύσις, -εως, ἡ, *nature*
φυτεύω, *I plant*

root *ΧΑΡ*, 'rejoice'

χαίρω, *I rejoice* (2nd aor. pass. ἐ-χάρ-ην)
συγχαίρω, *I rejoice with*
χαρά, -ᾶς, ἡ, *joy, delight*
χάρις, -ιτος, ἡ, *grace, favor*
χάριν, (accusative of the noun χάρις used absolutely, *in favor of, for the pleasure of*), preposition with the gen., *on account of, for the sake of*
χαρίζομαι, *I give freely, forgive*
χάρισμα, -ατος, τό, *a gift* (freely and graciously given)
εὐχαριστέω, *I give thanks*
εὐχαριστία, -ας, ἡ, *thanksgiving*

---

χιλιάς, -άδος, ἡ, *a thousand*
χίλιοι, -αι, -α, *a thousand*
χιλίαρχος, -ου, ὁ, *a military tribune, captain*
τετρακισχίλιοι, -αι, -α, *four thousand*
πεντακισχίλιοι, -αι, -α, *five thousand*

---

χράομαι, *I use*
χρεία, -ας, ἡ, *a need*
χρηστός, -ή, -όν, (*useful, good*), *mild, comfortable, gracious*
χρηστότης, -ητος, ἡ, *goodness, kindness*
χρήζω, *I have need of*
χρῆμα, -ατος, τό, (*whatever one uses, a thing*), *money*; plural, *riches*
χρηματίζω, (*I transact business*, hence, *consult, deliberate*), *I make answer*

71

(in an oracle), *I warn*; passive, *I am warned by God*; *I receive a name* (from my business), *am called*

---

χρυσός, -οῦ, ὁ, *gold*
χρυσίον, -ου, τό, *gold*
χρύσεος, -α, -ον, contracted χρυσοῦς, -ῆ, -οῦν, *golden*

---

χώρα, -ας, ἡ, *a country*
χωρίον, -ου, τό, *a place, field*
χωρέω, *I make room, hold*
ἀναχωρέω, *I depart*
χωρίζω, *I separate, depart*

---

ψεύδομαι, *I lie*
ψευδομαρτυρέω, *I testify falsely, bear false witness*
ψευδοπροφήτης, -ου, ὁ, *a false prophet*
ψεῦδος, -ους, τό, *a lie*
ψεύστης, -ου, ὁ, *a liar*

# THE INDO-EUROPEAN FAMILY
# OF LANGUAGES

LANGUAGES, like individuals, are related to each other in families. According to two independent estimates, there have been 2,796 languages in the world and these may be classified into about 26 families.[1] The family of languages that is of most interest to the student of New Testament Greek is the Indo-European family. Besides Greek this family includes seven other sub-families of languages, the Indo-Iranian, Armenian, Albanian, Italic, Celtic, Germanic, and Balto-Slavic. (See Table I on pp. 74 f.)

What region was the common center, the home of the parent tongue from which all the Indo-European languages have developed, has long been a subject of discussion.[2] Earlier investigators were confident that it was in Asia—the continent which was the source of the oldest civilization, the traditional site of the Garden of Eden, and the locality where Sanskrit was spoken. But more recently certain scholars have favored the hypothesis that localizes what is popularly called 'the cradle of the Aryans' in the region extending north of the Black Sea and Caucasia, and south and west of the Volga River.[3]

Beginning about 3000 B.C. it is probable that successive migrations of tribes left the old home and drifted, some south-east to the Ganges valley, others westward throughout Europe.[4] No remains of the parent Indo-European tongue are extant, but, by means of comparative linguistics, scholars have been able to reconstruct a large part of its vocabulary and grammar.[5]

---

[1] Louis H. Gray, *Foundations of Language* (New York, 1939), pp. 417 f. and 303.

[2] The question has not yet been satisfactorily answered; for significant discussions see F. Specht, 'Sprachliches zur Urheimat der Indogermanen' in Kuhn's *Zeitschrift für vergleichende Sprachforschung*, lxvi (1939), pp. 1–74, and Giacomo Devoto, *Origini indeuropee* (Florence, [1962]).

[3] See, e.g., Harold H. Bender, *The Home of the Indo-Europeans* (Princeton, 1922), and Gray, op. cit., pp. 304–10.

[4] Today all of the languages of Europe belong to the Indo-European family except Basque, Esthonian, Finnish, Hungarian, Lapp, and Turkish.

[5] Works of this kind are A. Walde and J. Pokorny, *Etymologisches Wörterbuch der*

TABLE I. THE INDO-EUROPEAN LANGUAGES

Extant modern languages are in the last column

| | | | | |
|---|---|---|---|---|
| INDO-IRANIAN | Indic | Vedic Sanskrit; Classical Sanskrit | Pāli, Prakrit dialects | Bengali Hindi Marathi Gujarati, etc. |
| | Iranian | Avestan Old Persian | Pahlavi Sogdian Sacian | Mod. Persian Kurdish Ossetan Afghan Baluchi, etc. |
| ARMENIAN | | | Old Armenian | Armenian |
| ALBANIAN | | | | Albanian |
| GREEK | East Greek | Attic-Ionic Arcadian-Cyprian Aeolic: Lesbian, Thessalian, Boeotian | The *koine* or Hellenistic Greek | Mod. Greek |
| | West Greek | NW Greek: Locrian, Phocian, Elean Doric: Laconian, Argolic, Corinthian, Cretan, etc. | | (Tsaconian dialect) |
| ITALIC | Latin-Faliscan | Latin Faliscan | Vulgar Latin | French Provençal Catalan Spanish Portuguese Italian Rhaeto-Roman Rumanian |
| | Oscan-Umbrian | Oscan Umbrian Paelignian Volscian, etc. | | |

Table I, continued

| | | | | |
|---|---|---|---|---|
| **CELTIC** | Gaelic | | Old Irish | Irish<br>Scotch Gaelic<br>Manx |
| | Britannic | | Old Welsh<br>Old Cornish<br>Old Breton | Welsh<br><br>Breton |
| | Continental | Celtic Inscriptions | | |
| **GERMANIC** | East Germanic | | Gothic | |
| | North Germanic | | Old Norse | Swedish<br>Danish<br>Norwegian<br>Icelandic |
| | West Germanic | Anglo-Frisian | Old English<br>Old Frisian | English<br>Frisian |
| | | German {Low / High} | Old Saxon<br>Old Low Franconian<br>Old High German | Dutch<br><br>German |
| **BALTO-SLAVIC** | Baltic | | Old Lithuanian<br>Old Lettic<br>Old Prussian | Lithuanian<br>Lettic |
| | Slavic | South Slavic | Old Church Slavic | Bulgarian<br>Serbo-Croatian<br>Slovenian |
| | | West Slavic | Polabian | Bohemian<br>Slovak<br>Polish<br>Wendish |
| | | East Slavic | | Great Russian<br>White Russian<br>Ukrainian |

From Carl D. Buck, *Comparative Grammar of Greek and Latin* (Chicago, 1937), pp. 3 f.

Several Anatolian languages of ancient Asia Minor (Hittite, Luwian, Palaic, Hieroglyphic Hittite, Lydian, Lycian) and Tocharian (A and B) of Central Asia also belong to the Indo-European family, but their exact relationships have not yet been fully determined.

75

The method and validity of comparative linguistics can be illustrated within one branch of the Indo-European family. The Romance languages are obviously related, for it can be observed that, within historic times, they have assumed their present forms in developing from their common source, the Latin language. Thus, for example, the Latin word *caballus*, meaning 'a pack-horse, a nag,' is the origin of Romance words for 'horse,' such as French *cheval*, Spanish *caballo*, Italian *cavallo*, Portuguese *cavalo*, Rumanian *cal*, Provençal and Catalan, *cavall*.[1] So, too, when the several sub-families of the extant Indo-European languages are compared, the hypothetical parent tongue may be reconstructed with a considerable degree of probability. Thus, the fact that the Greek word μήτηρ resembles the Sanskrit *mātár-*, Avestan (Old Persian) *mātā*, Old Armenian *mair*, Latin *māter*, Old High German *muoter* (modern German *Mutter*), Old Irish *māthir*, Old Slavic *mati*, etc., renders it highly probable that all these words have come from an Indo-European word *\*mātér-*.[2]

The words for 'horse' in the Romance languages, all of which have originated from the same Latin word, are said to be *cognate* to one another. So, too, besides words in English which are borrowed or derived from Greek (such as the derivatives supplied in Part I), other English words are said to be cognate to words in Greek. Cognate words, as their name indicates,[3] are words, in different languages, which are 'related' to each other because they have descended from the same ancestor. Although Greek and English have been separated from their common parent stock for so many centuries and have become widely different in so many respects, linguists have observed that some of the differences can be accounted for in terms of regular phonetic changes. Thus, because Greek and English are sister languages, it is possible to identify words in each which have descended from the same words in the primitive Indo-European speech. Jacob Grimm (1785–1863) formulated a statement of the mutation of consonants involved in the development

*indogermanischen Sprachen*, 3 vols. (Berlin and Leipzig, 1927–32), A. Meillet, *Introduction à l'étude comparative des langues indo-européennes*, 7th edn. (Paris, 1934), and H. Hirt, *Indogermanische Grammatik*, 7 vols. (Heidelberg, 1921–37).

[1] For still other dialectical forms, see W. Meyer-Lübke, *Romanisches etymologisches Wörterbuch*, 3rd edn. (Heidelberg, 1935), s.v. *caballus*.

[2] The asterisk signifies that this word does not appear in any historical source. For other derivations from this stem, see Walde–Pokorny, op. cit., s.v. *mātér-*.

[3] Latin *cognatus*, 'related (by blood).'

of the Teutonic languages.[1] (In all languages consonants are the skeleton-letters of words, for vowel-sounds are far from being as persistent—a fact which may be observed by noting the differing local pronunciations of the same words in our own language.)[2]

How Grimm's law operates is shown in the following table, which indicates what forms the consonants in the Greek group will assume in the English group, and illustrates them by a few examples. The Greek declensional terminations have, of course, no correspondence in the English words. Other words which might be thought to be exceptions to Grimm's law are accounted for by Grassmann's law and Verner's law.[3]

The consonants which are involved are those that form the so-called square of mutes:

|  | voiceless | voiced | aspirate |
| --- | --- | --- | --- |
| Labials (lip sounds) | π | β | φ |
| Dentals (teeth sounds) | τ | δ | θ |
| Palatals (palate sounds) | κ | γ | χ |

1. The voiceless stops, π, τ, κ, are represented in cognate English words by *f, th, h.*

(a) π and *f*                              *English cognate*
πατήρ 'father'                             *f*ather
πληγή 'stroke, blow'                       *f*lick, *f*log
πολύς, 'much'                              *f*ull, *f*ill,
πούς 'foot'                                *f*oot
πῦρ 'fire'                                 *f*ire

(b) τ and *th*
ὀδούς (stem ὀδόντ-) 'tooth'                too*th*
τρεῖς 'three'                              *th*ree

(c) κ and *h*
καρδία 'heart'                             *h*eart
καρπός 'fruit'                             *h*arvest
κύων (stem κυν-) 'dog'                      *h*ound

[1] For a most interesting account of the steps by which the present formulation of Grimm's law was attained, see Leonard Bloomfield's book entitled *Language* (New York, 1933), pp. 14 f. and 347–59.

[2] E.g. a man wears a 'doiby' hat in the Bronx, a 'darby' in Great Britain, and a 'derby' elsewhere.

[3] A succinct statement of these laws may be read in Webster's *New International Dictionary.*

2. The voiced stops, β, δ, γ, are represented in cognate English words by *p*, *t*, *k*.

(*a*) β and *p*  — *English cognate*
βύρσα 'a hide' — *p*urse
κύβος 'loin' — hi*p*

(*b*) δ and *t*
δρῦς 'oak' — *t*ree
δύο 'two' — *t*wo
ὀδόντ- 'tooth' — *t*ooth

(*c*) γ and *k*
γένος 'race, family' — *k*in
γόνυ 'knee' — *k*nee
γινώσκω (stem γνω-) 'know' — *k*now

3. The aspirated stops, φ, θ, χ, are represented in cognate English words by *b*, *d*, *g*.

(*a*) φ and *b* — *English cognate*
φέρω 'I bear' — *b*ear
φράτηρ 'a member of a brother-
    hood' — *b*rother

(*b*) θ and *d*
θυγάτηρ 'daughter' — *d*aughter
θύρα 'door' — *d*oor
μέθυ 'wine' — mea*d*
τίθημι (stem θε-) 'I put, place' — *d*o

(*c*) χ and *g*
ὀχέω 'I uphold, carry, ride' — weig*h*
χήν (dat. pl. χησί) 'goose' — *g*oose
χόρτος 'enclosure, grass' — *g*arden

# APPENDIX II

# PREPOSITIONS IN COMPOSITION
# WITH VERBS

ORIGINALLY a preposition was an auxiliary word which assisted in defining and clarifying the significance of the case of a noun.[1] When a preposition is compounded with a verb its primitive connotation may acquire various other functions and meanings. One of the most important of these is the so-called 'perfective' use of the preposition. When used in this way the preposition usually completes or emphasizes the action conveyed by the simple verb. All Indo-European languages employ prepositions in this perfectivizing sense. Compare, for example, the English verbs *bring* and *bring up*, *burn* and *burn up*, *carry* and *carry off*, *drink* and *drink up*, *eat* and *eat up*, *follow* and *follow up* or *follow through*, *go* and *go away*, *knock* and *knock down*, *make* and *make over*, *pluck* and *pluck out*, *speak* and *speak out*, *wake* and *wake up*, *work* and *work out*. In each instance the compound verb intensifies the sense of the simple verb. So too in Greek—although Greek and English do not always use the same preposition to convey the same idea. Compare ἐργάζομαι, *I work*, with κατεργάζομαι, *I work out* (literally *down to the finish*, see Phil. 2 : 12); καίομαι, *I burn*, with κατακαίομαι, *I burn up, burn completely* (see Matt. 3 : 12); ἐσθίω, *I eat*, with κατεσθίω, *I eat up, devour* (see Luke 20 : 47).[2]

In the following list each preposition is analyzed as to its principal meanings when in composition with verbs. Most of the semantic shifts are perfectly clear. Occasionally, however, the meaning of the compound verb cannot easily be determined from the separate meanings of its component parts. Thus, the force of ἀπό in ἀποκρίνομαι and in ἀποθνήσκω is no longer obvious. Perhaps originally the former verb meant 'I answer *back*' and the latter 'I die *off*'.

[1] See, further, A. T. Robertson, *A Grammar of the Greek New Testament in the Light of Historical Research*, 5th edn. (New York, 1931), pp. 553–7. The primary meanings of Greek prepositions used with various cases may be seen in Table II on p. 80.

[2] For additional information about perfective verbs see J. H. Moulton, *A Grammar of New Testament Greek*, vol. i, *Prolegomena*, 3rd edn. (Edinburgh, 1908), pp. 111–18.

# TABLE II. GEOMETRIC ARRANGEMENT OF THE GREEK PREPOSITIONS

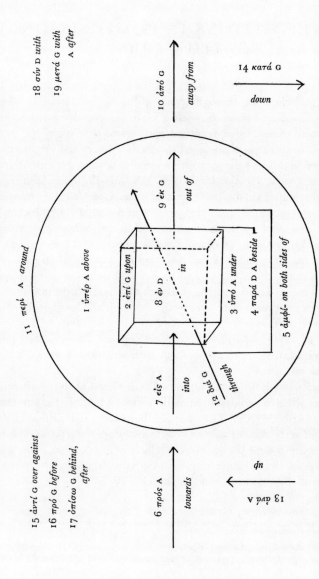

Notes: 1. The symbols, G, D, and A should be read: 'with the genitive case means,' 'with the dative case means,' and 'with the accusative case means.' Number 5 appears in the New Testament only in compound words.

2. Only the basic meanings of prepositions with certain cases are given here. For other meanings with other cases, a lexicon should be consulted.

It will be remembered that a preposition which ends in a vowel drops that vowel when compounded with a verb which begins with a vowel, as ἀπέρχομαι from ἀπό and ἔρχομαι. The only exceptions to this rule are compounds with περί and πρό, which do not drop their final vowel, as προάγω and περιάγω.

ἀνά  (1)  Root meaning *upwards*
ἀναβαίνω, *I go up*
ἀνίστημι, *I cause to stand up*

(2)  *Again, anew, thoroughly*
ἀναζάω, *I live again, revive*
ἀναπαύω, *I give rest to* (someone) *thoroughly, refresh*
ἀνασταυρόω, *I crucify afresh*

(3)  *Back, backwards, to and fro*
ἀναστρέφω, *I turn upside down, turn back, walk to and fro, conduct myself, live*
ἀναστροφή, '*walk*,' *conduct*

ἀντί  (1)  Root meaning *opposite, against, over against*
ἀντιπαρέρχομαι, *I pass by* [παρά] *on the other side*
ἀντιλέγω, *I speak against, oppose, resist*
ἀντίχριστος, *an opponent of Christ, antichrist*

(2)  *Requital*
ἀνταποδίδωμι, *I give back as an equivalent requital* (ἀντί expresses the idea of a full, complete return)
ἀντιμισθία, *reward, requital*

(3)  *Substitution*
ἀνθύπατος (ἀντί and ὕπατος, an alternative form of ὑπέρτατος, *supreme*), *a proconsul*
Perhaps ἀντίχριστος should be classified here as 'one who assumes the guise of Christ'

ἀπό  (1)  Root meaning *away from*
ἀπέρχομαι, *I depart from*
ἀποκαλύπτω, *I withdraw a cover from, uncover, reveal*

(2)  *Back again* (like Latin *re-*)
ἀποδίδωμι, *I give back, return*
ἀπολαμβάνω, *I take back, recover*

81

(3) *Perfective*

ἀπέχω, *I have fully, have received* (in full; see Matt. 6: 2, 5, 16); also in sense (1), *I am away, distant*; middle, *I hold myself off from, abstain*

ἀπόλλυμι, *I destroy utterly*; middle, *I perish completely*

ἀπολούομαι, *I wash myself thoroughly*

διά (1) Root meaning *through*

διέρχομαι, *I go through, pass through*

(2) *Distribution*

διαγγέλλω, *I publish abroad, proclaim*

διαδίδωμι, *I distribute*

(3) *Transition, change*

διαβάλλω, *I throw across, slander*

διαλλάσσω, *I change* (make other [ἄλλος] than), *reconcile*

(4) *Separation*

διασπάω, *I tear apart*

(5) *Perfective*

διαβεβαιόομαι, *I assert confidently, emphatically*

διακαθαρίζω, *I cleanse thoroughly*

διαφυλάσσω, *I guard carefully*

εἰς Root meaning *into*

εἰσέρχομαι, *I go into, enter*

ἐκ (1) Root meaning *from out of*

ἐκβάλλω, *I cast out*

ἐξέρχομαι, *I go out*

(2) *Perfective*

ἐκπληρόω, *I fill completely*

ἐξαπορέομαι, *I am utterly at a loss*

ἐν (1) Root meaning *in*

ἐνοικέω, *I dwell in*

(2) Motion *into*

ἐμβαίνω, *I step into* [a boat], *I embark*

ἐπί (1) Root meaning *on, upon*
ἐπιβάλλω, *I cast, lay,* or *put upon*
ἐπιτίθημι, *I lay, set,* or *place upon*

(2) Motion *towards*
ἐπέρχομαι, *I come upon* (sometimes with hostility)
ἐπιβάλλω, *I lay* or *put upon*

(3) *Upwards*
ἐπαίρω, *I lift up, raise*

(4) *Superintendence*
ἐπίσκοπος, *one who oversees, a bishop*
ἐπιστάτης, *one who is set over, a master*

κατά (1) Root meaning *down from, down*
καταβαίνω, *I go down*

(2) *Opposition*
κατακρίνω, *I give judgment against, condemn*
καταράομαι, *I pray against, curse*

(3) In succession, *in order*
καταρτίζω, *I set in order, mend*
κατευθύνω, *I make straight, guide, direct*

(4) *After, behind*
κατακολουθέω, *I follow after*
καταλείπω, *I leave behind, forsake*

(5) *Perfective*
κατεργάζομαι, *I work out thoroughly, accomplish*
κατεσθίω, *I eat up, devour*

μετά (1) Root meaning *association with*
μεταδίδωμι, *I share* (a thing) *with* (anyone), *impart*
μετέχω, *I partake of, share in*

(2) *Change, alteration*
μεταβαίνω, *I pass from one place to another, depart*
μεταμορφόω, *I change to another form, transform, transfigure*
μετανοέω, *I change my mind* or *purpose, repent*

(3) *After, in search of*
μεταπέμπω, *I send after* or *for, summon*

83

παρά (1) Root meaning *beside, near*
παραγίνομαι, *I am at hand, arrive*
παρακαλέω, *I call to my side, summon, admonish, entreat, encourage, comfort*

(2) *Violation, transgression, neglect*
παραβαίνω, *I go by the side of* (and beyond), *overstep, transgress*
παρακούω, *I hear amiss, hear without heeding, disobey*

περί (1) Root meaning *in a circuit about, around*
περιβάλλω, *I throw around, I clothe*
περιπατέω, *I walk about,* Hebraistically, in an ethical sense, *I conduct myself, live*

(2) *Beyond* (because that which surrounds a thing does not belong to the thing itself but is beyond it)
περισσεύω, *I exceed* (the ordinary, the necessary), *I abound, cause to abound*

πρό Root meaning *before* (of place or time), *forth*
προάγω, *I lead forth, go before*
προγινώσκω, *I know beforehand, foreknow*
προφητεύω, *I foretell, speak forth, prophesy*

πρός (1) Root meaning *to, towards*
προσέρχομαι, *I come to, approach*
προσέχω, *I bring to*; with τὸν νοῦν, *I turn my mind to, attend to, give heed to*
προσκυνέω, *I make obeisance to* one (in token of reverence), *fall down before, worship*

(2) *On, at*
προσκόπτω, *I strike* (the hand or foot) *against, stumble at*

σύν (1) Root meaning *together with*
συνάγω, *I gather together*
συνεργέω, *I work together*
συνίημι, (*I bring together in my mind*), *I understand*

(2) *Perfective*
συνθρύπτω, *I break in pieces, crush utterly*
συνκαλύπτω, *I veil (cover) completely*
συντηρέω, *I keep safe*

84

ὑπέρ Root meaning *over, above*

    ὑπερβάλλω, (*I throw over* or *beyond*), *I exceed, surpass*

    ὑπερέχω, (*I have* or *hold over*), *I am superior, excel*

    ὑπερνικάω, *I am more than a conqueror*


ὑπό Root meaning *under*, hence of subjection and compliance

    ὑποδέομαι, *I bind under* (the foot)

    ὑπομένω, (*I remain under*), *I remain, persevere, endure*

    ὑπάγω, (*I lead under*), *I withdraw myself, depart*

|  | DEMONSTRATIVE | INTERROGATIVE | INDEFINITE | RELATIVE and/or INDEFINITE RELATIVE |
|---|---|---|---|---|
| SIMPLE | ὅδε, this (here)<br>οὗτος, this (near)<br>ἐκεῖνος, that (yonder) | τίς; who? which? what? | τις, someone, anyone | ὅς, who, which<br>ὅστις, whoever, whichever |
| PLACE | αὐτοῦ, here, there<br>ὧδε, hither, here | ποῦ; where? | πού, somewhere | οὗ, where, whither<br>ὅπου, where, whither |
|  | ἐντεῦθεν, hence<br>ἐκεῖθεν, thence | πόθεν; whence? |  | ὅθεν, whence |
|  | ἐκεῖ, there<br>ἐνθάδε, here, hither |  |  |  |
| MANNER | οὕτως, thus, so | πῶς; how? | πώς, at all, somehow, in any way | ὡς, as, about |
| TIME | νῦν and νυνί, now<br>τότε, then | πότε; when? | ποτέ, at some time, once, ever | ὅτε, when<br>ὅταν, whenever, when |
| QUANTITY | τοσοῦτος, so great, so much | πόσος; how great? how much? |  | ὅσος, as great as, as much as |
| QUALITY | τοιοῦτος, of such a kind, such | ποῖος; of what sort? what? |  | οἷος, such as<br>ὁποῖος, of what sort |
| SIZE | τηλικοῦτος, so large, so great | πηλίκος; how large? how great? |  | ἡλίκος, what size of |

# APPENDIX IV

# PRINCIPAL PARTS OF SOME IMPORTANT VERBS

THE following list of principal parts is a summary of some of the important verbs in the New Testament. The seven irregular verbs which are given above on page 46 have not been repeated here. The enclosing of a principal part in parentheses signifies that no form of the tense system immediately derived from that part occurs in the New Testament. In some instances, however, compound verbs which involve that principal part are found in the New Testament. Because of the exigencies of space the definitions of these verbs have been severely limited.

| PRESENT | FUTURE | AORIST | PERFECT ACTIVE | PERFECT MIDDLE | AORIST PASSIVE |
|---|---|---|---|---|---|
| ἀγαπάω love | ἀγαπήσω | ἠγάπησα | ἠγάπηκα | ἠγάπημαι | ἠγαπήθην |
| ἄγω lead | ἄξω | ἤγαγον ἦξα | (ἦχα) | ἦγμαι | ἤχθην |
| αἴρω take up, take away | ἀρῶ | ἦρα | ἦρκα | ἦρμαι | ἤρθην |
| αἰτέω ask for | αἰτήσω | ᾔτησα | ᾔτηκα | (ᾔτημαι) | ᾐτήθην |
| ἀκούω hear | ἀκούσω | ἤκουσα | ἀκήκοα | (ἤκουσμαι) | ἠκούσθην |
| ἁμαρτάνω sin | ἁμαρτήσω | ἡμάρτησα ἥμαρτον | ἡμάρτηκα | (ἡμάρτημαι) | (ἡμαρτήθην) |
| ἀνοίγω open | ἀνοίξω | ἀνέῳξα ἤνοιξα ἠνέῳξα | ἀνέῳγα | ἀνέῳγμαι ἠνέῳγμαι ἤνοιγμαι | ἀνεῳχθην ἠνοίχθην ἠνεῳχθην |
| ἀπόλλυμι destroy | ἀπολέσω ἀπολῶ | ἀπώλεσα | ἀπόλωλα | | |
| ἀποστέλλω send (with a commission) | ἀποστελῶ | ἀπέστειλα | ἀπέσταλκα | ἀπέσταλμαι | ἀπεστάλην |
| ἀφίημι let go; forgive | ἀφήσω | ἀφῆκα | ἀφεῖκα | ἀφεῖμαι | ἀφέθην |
| βάλλω throw, put | βαλῶ | ἔβαλον ἔβαλα | βέβληκα | βέβλημαι | ἐβλήθην |

87

| PRESENT | FUTURE | AORIST | PERFECT ACTIVE | PERFECT MIDDLE | AORIST PASSIVE |
|---|---|---|---|---|---|
| γεννάω beget | γεννήσω | ἐγέννησα | γεγέννηκα | γεγέννημαι | ἐγεννήθην |
| γίνομαι become | γενήσομαι | ἐγενόμην | γέγονα | γεγένημαι | ἐγενήθην |
| γινώσκω know | γνώσομαι | ἔγνων | ἔγνωκα | ἔγνωσμαι | ἐγνώσθην |
| γράφω write | γράψω | ἔγραψα | γέγραφα | γέγραμμαι | ἐγράφην |
| δείκνυμι show | δείξω | ἔδειξα | (δέδειχα) | δέδειγμαι | ἐδείχθην |
| δίδωμι give | δώσω | ἔδωκα | δέδωκα | δέδομαι | ἐδόθην |
| διώκω pursue, persecute | διώξω | ἐδίωξα | (δεδίωχα) | δεδίωγμαι | ἐδιώχθην |
| δοξάζω glorify | δοξάσω | ἐδόξασα | (δεδόξακα) | δεδόξασμαι | ἐδοξάσθην |
| ἐγείρω raise up | ἐγερῶ | ἤγειρα | | ἐγήγερμαι | ἠγέρθην |
| ἐλέγχω convict, reprove | ἐλέγξω | ἤλεγξα | | | ἠλέγχθην |
| ἐλεέω pity | ἐλεήσω | ἠλέησα | (ἠλέηκα) | ἠλέημαι | ἠλεήθην |
| ἐλπίζω hope | ἐλπιῶ | ἤλπισα | ἤλπικα | | |
| ἐρωτάω ask | ἐρωτήσω | ἠρώτησα | (ἠρώτηκα) | (ἠρώτημαι) | (ἠρωτήθην) |
| ἑτοιμάζω prepare | ἑτοιμάσω | ἡτοίμασα | ἡτοίμακα | ἡτοίμασμαι | ἡτοιμάσθην |
| εὐαγγελίζω preach the Gospel | (εὐαγγελίσω) | εὐηγγέλισα | (εὐηγγέλικα) | εὐηγγέλισμαι | εὐηγγελίσθην |
| εὐλογέω bless | εὐλογήσω | εὐλόγησα | εὐλόγηκα | εὐλόγημαι | εὐλογήθην |
| εὑρίσκω find | εὑρήσω | εὗρον | εὕρηκα | (εὕρημαι) | εὑρέθην |
| ἔχω have, hold | ἕξω | ἔσχον | ἔσχηκα | | |
| ἥκω have come | ἥξω | ἧξα | ἧκα | | |
| θαυμάζω marvel | θαυμάσομαι | ἐθαύμασα | (τεθαύμακα) | | ἐθαυμάσθην |
| θεραπεύω heal | θεραπεύσω | ἐθεράπευσα | (τεθεράπευκα) | τεθεράπευμαι | ἐθεραπεύθην |

88

| PRESENT | FUTURE | AORIST | PERFECT ACTIVE | PERFECT MIDDLE | AORIST PASSIVE |
|---|---|---|---|---|---|
| θύω *sacrifice* | | ἔθυσα | | τέθυμαι | ἐτύθην |
| ἵστημι *stand* | στήσω | ἔστησα ἔστην | ἔστηκα | (ἔσταμαι) | ἐστάθην |
| καθαρίζω *cleanse* | καθαριῶ | ἐκαθάρισα | | κεκαθάρισμαι | ἐκαθαρίσθην |
| καλέω *call* | καλέσω | ἐκάλεσα | κέκληκα | κέκλημαι | ἐκλήθην |
| κηρύσσω *proclaim* | κηρύξω | ἐκήρυξα | (κεκήρυχα) | (κεκήρυγμαι) | ἐκηρύχθην |
| κρίνω *judge* | κρινῶ | ἔκρινα | κέκρικα | κέκριμαι | ἐκρίθην |
| λαλέω *speak* | λαλήσω | ἐλάλησα | λελάληκα | λελάλημαι | ἐλαλήθην |
| λαμβάνω *take, receive* | λήμψομαι | ἔλαβον | εἴληφα | εἴλημμαι | ἐλήμφθην |
| λείπω *leave* | λείψω | ἔλιπον | (λέλοιπα) | λέλειμμαι | ἐλείφθην |
| λύω *loose* | λύσω | ἔλυσα | (λέλυκα) | λέλυμαι | ἐλύθην |
| μαρτυρέω *bear witness* | μαρτυρήσω | ἐμαρτύρησα | μεμαρτύρηκα | μεμαρτύρημαι | ἐμαρτυρήθην |
| μένω *remain* | μενῶ | ἔμεινα | μεμένηκα | | |
| ξηραίνω *dry up* | | ἐξήρανα | | ἐξήραμμαι | ἐξηράνθην |
| οἰκοδομέω *build, edify* | οἰκοδομήσω | ᾠκοδόμησα | | ᾠκοδόμημαι | ᾠκοδομήθην |
| πάσχω *suffer* | (πείσομαι) | ἔπαθον | πέπονθα | | |
| πείθω *persuade* | πείσω | ἔπεισα | πέποιθα | πέπεισμαι | ἐπείσθην |
| πειράζω *tempt* | (πειράσω) | ἐπείρασα | (πεπείρακα) | πεπείρασμαι | ἐπειράσθην |
| πέμπω *send* | πέμψω | ἔπεμψα | (πέπομφα) | (πέπεμμαι) | ἐπέμφθην |
| πίνω *drink* | πίομαι | ἔπιον | πέπωκα | (πέπομαι) | (ἐπόθην) |
| πίπτω *fall* | πεσοῦμαι | ἔπεσον ἔπεσα | πέπτωκα | | |
| πιστεύω *believe* | (πιστεύσω) | ἐπίστευσα | πεπίστευκα | πεπίστευμαι | ἐπιστεύθην |

89

| PRESENT | FUTURE | AORIST | PERFECT ACTIVE | PERFECT MIDDLE | AORIST PASSIVE |
|---|---|---|---|---|---|
| πληρόω *fill, fulfill* | πληρώσω | ἐπλήρωσα | πεπλήρωκα | πεπλήρωμαι | ἐπληρώθην |
| ποιέω *do, make* | ποιήσω | ἐποίησα | πεποίηκα | πεποίημαι | (ἐποιήθην) |
| πράσσω *do, perform* | πράξω | ἔπραξα | πέπραχα | πέπραγμαι | |
| σπείρω *sow* | (σπερῶ) | ἔσπειρα | | ἔσπαρμαι | ἐσπάρην |
| σταυρόω *crucify* | σταυρώσω | ἐσταύρωσα | (ἐσταύρωκα) | ἐσταύρωμαι | ἐσταυρώθην |
| στηρίζω *strengthen* | στηρίξω στηρίσω | ἐστήριξα ἐστήρισα | | ἐστήριγμαι | ἐστηρίχθην |
| στρέφω *turn* | (στρέψω) | ἔστρεψα | | (ἔστραμμαι) | ἐστράφην |
| σῴζω *save* | σώσω | ἔσωσα | σέσωκα | σέσωσμαι σέσωμαι | ἐσώθην |
| τελέω *finish, fulfill* | (τελέσω) | ἐτέλεσα | τετέλεκα | τετέλεσμαι | ἐτελέσθην |
| τηρέω *keep* | τηρήσω | ἐτήρησα | τετήρηκα | τετήρημαι | ἐτηρήθην |
| τίθημι *place, put* | θήσω | ἔθηκα | τέθεικα | τέθειμαι | ἐτέθην |
| τιμάω *value, honor* | τιμήσω | ἐτίμησα | (τετίμηκα) | τετίμημαι | (ἐτιμήθην) |
| φανερόω *make manifest* | φανερώσω | ἐφανέρωσα | (πεφανέρωκα) | πεφανέρωμαι | ἐφανερώθην |
| φιλέω *love* | (φιλήσω) | ἐφίλησα | πεφίληκα | (πεφίλημαι) | (ἐφιλήθην) |
| χαίρω *rejoice* | χαρήσομαι | | | | ἐχάρην |

90

# APPENDIX V

# FEMININE NOUNS OF THE SECOND DECLENSION

THE beginner in Greek learns that, with a very few exceptions, nouns of the second declension ending in -ος are masculine in gender. The exceptions that occur most frequently in the New Testament are ἡ ὁδός and ἡ ἔρημος. Besides these two words, however, there are— surprisingly enough—thirty-three additional feminine nouns of the second declension in the New Testament, as well as eighteen other nouns of the second declension that are sometimes masculine and sometimes feminine. Examples of the second group include παρθένος and θεός; the former word, which is usually feminine, is masculine in Revelation 14 : 4, and the latter word is feminine in Acts 19 :37, where it refers to the goddess Artemis (sometimes called Diana).

In several cases what now functions as a noun was originally an adjective of two terminations used with a feminine noun. In the course of time, however, the latter came to be omitted, and the adjective alone was felt to be sufficient. For example, the adjective ἄβυσσος, -ον, means *bottomless*; ἡ ἄβυσσος (supply χώρα, *place*) means *the bottomless place*, hence *the abyss*.

In the following lists the numeral which follows the definition indicates the number of times that the Greek noun appears in the New Testament.

## A. *Feminine Nouns of the Second Declension*

ἄβυσσος, -ου, ἡ, *the abyss* (9)
ἀμέθυστος, -ου, ἡ, *an amethyst* (1)
ἄμμος, -ου, ἡ, *sand* (5)
ἄμπελος, -ου, ἡ, *a vine* (9)
βάσανος, -ου, ἡ, *pain, torment* (3)
βίβλος, -ου, ἡ, *a book* (10)
βύσσος, -ου, ἡ, *linen* (1)
διάλεκτος, -ου, ἡ, *a language* (6)
διέξοδος, -ου, ἡ, *a thoroughfare* (1)

δοκός, -οῦ, ἡ, a beam, a log (6)
εἴσοδος, -ου, ἡ, an entrance (5)
ἔξοδος, -ου, ἡ, a departure (3)
ἔρημος, -ου, ἡ, a desert, wilderness (as a substantive, 34)
καλλιέλαιος, -ου, ἡ, a cultivated olive tree (1)
κάμινος, -ου, ὁ, ἡ, a furnace (4)
κέδρος, -ου, ἡ, a cedar (1)
κιβωτός, -οῦ, ἡ, a box, ark (6)
νάρδος, -ου, ἡ, nard (2)
νῆσος, -ου, ἡ, an island (9)
νόσος, -ου, ἡ, a disease (11)
ὁδός, -οῦ, ἡ, a way, road, journey (101)
παράλιος, -ου, ἡ, a level place (1)
πάροδος, -ου, ἡ, a passing (1)
ῥάβδος, -ου, ἡ, a staff, rod (12)
'Ρόδος, -ου, ἡ, (the island of) Rhodes (1)
σάπφειρος, -ου, ἡ, a sapphire (1)
σορός, -οῦ, ἡ, a coffin (1)
σποδός, -οῦ, ἡ, ashes (3)
στάμνος, -ου, ἡ, a jar (1)
συκάμινος, -ου, ἡ, a sycamine tree (1)
τρίβος, -ου, ἡ, a path (3)
τροφός, -οῦ, ἡ, a nurse (1)
ὕσσωπος, -ου, ἡ, hyssop (2)
χαλκολίβανος, -ου, ἡ, burnished bronze (2)
ψῆφος, -ου, ἡ, a pebble, stone; a vote (3)

## B. Nouns of the Second Declension, Sometimes Masculine, Sometimes Feminine

ἀλάβαστρος, -ου, ὁ, ἡ, (is also sometimes neuter), an alabaster jar (4)
ἄρκος, -ου, ὁ, ἡ, a bear (1)
ἄψινθος, -ου, ὁ, ἡ, wormwood (2)
βάτος, -ου, ὁ, ἡ, a thorn or bramble-bush (4)
βήρυλλος, -ου, ὁ, ἡ, beryl (1)
διάκονος, -ου, ὁ, ἡ, a servant, deacon (29)
θεός, -οῦ, ὁ, ἡ, God, a god, a goddess (1314)
θυρωρός, -οῦ, ὁ, ἡ, a doorkeeper, janitor (4)
κάμηλος, -ου, ὁ, ἡ, a camel (6)
ληνός, -οῦ, ἡ, rarely ὁ, a wine press (4)

λίβανος, -ου, ὁ, rarely ἡ, *frankincense* (2)
λιμός, -οῦ, ὁ, rarely ἡ, *hunger, famine* (12)
μάρμαρος, -ου, ὁ, ἡ, *marble* (1)
νεωκόρος, -ου, ὁ, ἡ, *a temple keeper* (1)
ὄνος, -ου, ὁ, ἡ, *an ass* (6)
παρθένος, -ου, ὁ, ἡ, *a virgin* (15)
σμάραγδος, -ου, ὁ, ἡ, *an emerald* (1)
συγκληρονόμος, -ου, ὁ, ἡ, *a fellow heir, joint heir* (4)

# INDEX OF GREEK WORDS

The numerals refer to pages of the Frequency Word Lists

| | | | |
|---|---|---|---|
| γένος 26 | διαμερίζω 36 | εἰμί 7 | ἐνιαυτός 32 |
| γεύομαι 30 | διάνοια 35 | εἶπον 7 | ἔνοχος 39 |
| γεωργός 27 | διατάσσω 29 | εἰρήνη 13 | ἐντέλλομαι 30 |
| γῆ 9 | διατρίβω 39 | εἰς 8 | ἐντολή 15 |
| γίνομαι 7 | διαφέρω 33 | εἷς 9 | ἐνώπιον 14 |
| γινώσκω 9 | διδασκαλία 26 | εἰσάγω 37 | ἕξ 33 |
| γλῶσσα 16 | διδάσκαλος 16 | εἰσέρχομαι 10 | ἐξάγω 35 |
| γνωρίζω 23 | διδάσκω 13 | εἰσπορεύομαι 27 | ἐξαποστέλλω 34 |
| γνῶσις 22 | διδαχή 21 | εἶτα 33 | ἐξέρχομαι 9 |
| γνωστός 31 | δίδωμι 9 | ἐκ 8 | ἔξεστι 21 |
| γονεύς 26 | διέρχομαι 19 | ἕκαστος 14 | ἐξίστημι 29 |
| γόνυ 35 | δίκαιος 14 | ἑκατόν 29 | ἐξομολογέομαι 39 |
| γράμμα 32 | δικαιοσύνη 13 | ἑκατοντάρχης 26 | ἐξουθενέω 35 |
| γραμματεύς 15 | δικαιόω 19 | ἐκβάλλω 14 | ἐξουσία 12 |
| γραφή 16 | δικαίωμα 39 | ἐκεῖ 13 | ἔξω 15 |
| γράφω 10 | δίκτυον 35 | ἐκεῖθεν 23 | ἔξωθεν 34 |
| γρηγορέω 24 | διό 16 | ἐκεῖνος 9 | ἑορτή 23 |
| γυμνός 31 | διότι 24 | ἐκκλησία 12 | ἐπαγγελία 16 |
| γυνή 9 | διψάω 29 | ἐκκόπτω 39 | ἐπαγγέλλομαι 31 |
| | διωγμός 39 | ἐκλέγομαι 26 | ἔπαινος 37 |
| δαιμονίζομαι 33 | διώκω 18 | ἐκλεκτός 24 | ἐπαίρω 27 |
| δαιμόνιον 15 | δοκέω 15 | ἐκπίπτω 39 | ἐπαισχύνομαι 37 |
| δάκρυ 36 | δοκιμάζω 25 | ἐκπλήσσομαι 33 | ἐπάνω 27 |
| δέ 7 | δόλος 36 | ἐκπορεύομαι 20 | ἐπαύριον 29 |
| δέησις 27 | δόξα 10 | ἐκτείνω 30 | ἐπεί 22 |
| δεῖ 12 | δοξάζω 16 | ἕκτος 32 | ἐπειδή 39 |
| δεικνύω 20 | δουλεύω 23 | ἐκχέω 30 | ἔπειτα 30 |
| δεῖπνον 29 | δοῦλος 11 | ἐκχύννομαι 37 | ἐπερωτάω 16 |
| δέκα 23 | δράκων 33 | ἐλαία 31 | ἐπί 8 |
| δένδρον 23 | δύναμαι 9 | ἔλαιον 37 | ἐπιβάλλω 27 |
| δεξιός 16 | δύναμις 12 | ἐλάχιστος 32 | ἐπίγνωσις 26 |
| δέομαι 25 | δυνατός 20 | ἐλέγχω 28 | ἐπιγινώσκω 18 |
| δέρω 31 | δύο 11 | ἐλεέω 21 | ἐπιδίδωμι 39 |
| δέσμιος 29 | δώδεκα 14 | ἐλεημοσύνη 33 | ἐπιζητέω 34 |
| δεσμός 27 | δωρεά 36 | ἔλεος 23 | ἐπιθυμέω 30 |
| δεσπότης 39 | δῶρον 27 | ἐλευθερία 37 | ἐπιθυμία 19 |
| δεῦτε 35 | | ἐλεύθερός 25 | ἐπικαλέω 21 |
| δεύτερος 18 | ἐάν 9 | ἐλπίζω 21 | ἐπιλαμβάνομαι 27 |
| δέχομαι 16 | ἑαυτοῦ 9 | ἐλπίς 16 | ἐπιμένω 29 |
| δέω 18 | ἐάω 36 | ἐμαυτοῦ 20 | ἐπιπίπτω 34 |
| δηνάριον 29 | ἐγγίζω 18 | ἐμβαίνω 28 | ἐπισκέπτομαι 37 |
| διά 7 | ἐγγύς 21 | ἐμβλέπω 37 | ἐπίσταμαι 32 |
| διάβολος 20 | ἐγείρω 11 | ἐμός 14 | ἐπιστολή 24 |
| διαθήκη 20 | ἐγκαταλείπω 39 | ἐμπαίζω 33 | ἐπιστρέφω 39 |
| διακονέω 20 | ἐγώ 7 | ἔμπροσθεν 17 | ἐπιτάσσω 39 |
| διακονία 20 | ἔθνος 10 | ἐμφανίζω 39 | ἐπιτελέω 39 |
| διάκονος 22 | ἔθος 35 | ἐν 8 | ἐπιτίθημι 19 |
| διακρίνω 27 | εἰ 9 | ἔνατος 39 | ἐπιτιμάω 21 |
| διαλέγομαι 33 | εἶδον 9 | ἐνδείκνυμαι 37 | ἐπιτρέπω 28 |
| διαλογίζομαι 29 | εἴδωλον 37 | ἐνδύω 22 | ἐπουράνιος 27 |
| διαλογισμός 32 | εἴκοσι 37 | ἕνεκα 23 | ἑπτά 14 |
| διαμαρτύρομαι 31 | εἰκών 24 | ἐνεργέω 26 | ἐργάζομαι 19 |

ἐργάτης 30
ἔργον 10
ἔρημος 17
ἔρχομαι 8
ἐρῶ 13
ἐρωτάω 16
ἐσθίω 10
ἔσχατος 16
ἔσωθεν 35
ἕτερος 13
ἔτι 14
ἑτοιμάζω 19
ἕτοιμος 29
ἔτος 17
εὐαγγελίζω 16
εὐαγγέλιον 14
εὐδοκέω 26
εὐθέως 20
εὐθύς 16
εὐλογέω 18
εὐλογία 30
εὑρίσκω 10
εὐσέβεια 31
εὐφραίνω 32
εὐχαριστέω 19
εὐχαριστία 31
ἐφίστημι 26
ἐχθρός 21
ἔχω 8
ἕως 11

ζάω 11
ζῆλος 30
ζηλόω 37
ζητέω 12
ζύμη 34
ζωή 11
ζῷον 25
ζωοποιέω 37

ἤ 9
ἡγεμών 27
ἡγέομαι 22
ἤδη 16
ἥκω 23
ἥλιος 21
ἡμέρα 9

θάλασσα 13
θάνατος 12
θανατόω 37
θάπτω 37

θαυμάζω 18
θεάομαι 25
θέλημα 15
θέλω 9
θεμέλιος 30
θεός 8
θεραπεύω 18
θερίζω 26
θερισμός 34
θεωρέω 17
θηρίον 18
θησαυρός 29
θλίβω 39
θλίψις 18
θρίξ 31
θρόνος 16
θυγάτηρ 23
θυμός 28
θύρα 19
θυσία 22
θυσιαστήριον 25
θύω 34

ἰάομαι 23
ἰδέ 22
ἴδιος 12
ἱερεύς 21
ἱερόν 14
ἱκανός 19
ἱμάτιον 15
ἵνα 8
ἵππος 29
ἵστημι 10
ἰσχυρός 22
ἰσχύς 39
ἰσχύω 22
ἰχθύς 26

καθάπερ 29
καθαρίζω 21
καθαρός 23
καθεύδω 25
κάθημαι 14
καθίζω 17
καθίστημι 25
καθώς 10
καί 8
καινός 19
καιρός 14
καίω 35
κἀκεῖ 35
κἀκεῖθεν 39

κακία 37
κακός 17
κακῶς 30
κάλαμος 35
καλέω 11
καλός 13
καλῶς 20
καπνός 34
καρδία 10
καρπός 15
κατά 8
καταβαίνω 14
καταβολή 37
καταγγέλλω 28
καταισχύνω 34
κατακαίω 34
κατάκειμαι 35
κατακρίνω 28
καταλαμβάνω 31
καταλείπω 24
καταλύω 29
κατανοέω 32
καταντάω 34
καταργέω 23
καταρτίζω 34
κατασκευάζω 37
κατεργάζομαι 25
κατέρχομαι 30
κατεσθίω 31
κατέχω 28
κατηγορέω 24
κατοικέω 18
κάτω 37
καυχάομαι 21
καύχημα 37
καύχησις 37
κεῖμαι 24
κελεύω 23
κενός 28
κέρας 37
κερδαίνω 29
κεφαλή 14
κηρύσσω 15
κλάδος 37
κλαίω 19
κλάω 31
κλείω 30
κλέπτης 30
κλέπτω 34
κληρονομέω 28
κληρονομία 32
κληρονόμος 31

κλῆρος 37
κλῆσις 37
κλητός 37
κοιλία 25
κοιμάομαι 28
κοινός 32
κοινόω 32
κοινωνία 27
κοινωνός 39
κολλάομαι 35
κομίζω 35
κοπιάω 25
κόπος 28
κοσμέω 39
κόσμος 10
κράβαττος 37
κράζω 16
κρατέω 17
κράτος 35
κρείσσων 27
κρίμα 22
κρίνω 12
κρίσις 17
κριτής 27
κρυπτός 28
κρύπτω 26
κτίζω 31
κτίσις 27
κύριος 8
κωλύω 25
κώμη 23
κωφός 32

λαλέω 9
λαμβάνω 9
λαός 11
λατρεύω 26
λέγω 8
λευκός 25
λῃστής 31
λίαν 35
λίθος 17
λίμνη 37
λιμός 35
λογίζομαι 19
λόγος 9
λοιπός 16
λυπέω 23
λύπη 31
λυχνία 35
λύχνος 32
λύω 18

97

| | | | |
|---|---|---|---|
| μαθητής 9 | ναί 21 | ὄντως 40 | παράδοσις 34 |
| μακάριος 17 | ναός 18 | ὀπίσω 20 | παραιτέομαι 35 |
| μακράν 39 | νεανίσκος 37 | ὅπου 14 | παρακαλέω 12 |
| μακρόθεν 32 | νεκρός 10 | ὅπως 17 | παράκλησις 22 |
| μακροθυμέω 39 | νέος 25 | ὅραμα 35 | παραλαμβάνω 17 |
| μακροθυμία 32 | νεφέλη 24 | ὁράω 12 | παραλυτικος 37 |
| μάλιστα 35 | νήπιος 31 | ὀργή 20 | παράπτωμα 26 |
| μᾶλλον 14 | νηστεύω 27 | ὅρια 35 | παρατίθημι 27 |
| μανθάνω 23 | νικάω 23 | ὅρκος 40 | παράχρημα 28 |
| μαρτυρέω 14 | νίπτω 29 | ὅρος 15 | πάρειμι 30 |
| μαρτυρία 20 | νοέω 33 | ὅς, ἥ, ὅ 8 | παρεμβολή 37 |
| μαρτύριον 26 | νομίζω 31 | ὅσος 12 | παρέρχομαι 21 |
| μάρτυς 20 | νομικός 39 | ὅστις 10 | παρέχω 30 |
| μάχαιρα 22 | νόμος 10 | ὅταν 11 | παρθένος 31 |
| μέγας 10 | νόσος 37 | ὅτε 12 | παρίστημι 19 |
| μέλει 39 | νοῦς 24 | ὅτι 8 | παρουσία 24 |
| μέλλω 12 | νυμφίος 29 | οὐ 8 | παρρησία 21 |
| μέλος 21 | νῦν 11 | οὗ 24 | πᾶς 8 |
| μέν 10 | νυνί 25 | οὐαί 19 | πάσχα 22 |
| μένω 12 | νύξ 15 | οὐδέ 11 | πάσχω 19 |
| μερίζω 32 | | οὐδείς 9 | πατάσσω 40 |
| μεριμνάω 27 | ξενίζω 39 | οὐδέποτε 30 | πατήρ 9 |
| μέρος 18 | ξένος 32 | οὐκέτι 17 | παύομαι 31 |
| μέσος 16 | ξηραίνω 31 | οὖν 9 | πείθω 17 |
| μετά 9 | ξύλον 26 | οὔπω 22 | πεινάω 25 |
| μεταβαίνω 37 | ὁ, ἡ, τό 8 | οὐρανός 9 | πειράζω 20 |
| μετανοέω 20 | ὅδε 40 | οὖς 20 | πειρασμός 26 |
| μετάνοια 25 | ὁδός 12 | οὔτε 13 | πέμπω 14 |
| μέτρον 32 | ὁδούς 35 | οὗτος 8 | πενθέω 40 |
| μέχρι 27 | ὅθεν 31 | οὕτως 9 | πέντε 20 |
| μή 8 | οἶδα 9 | οὐχί 16 | περάν 25 |
| μηδέ 17 | οἰκία 13 | ὀφείλω 20 | περί 9 |
| μηδείς 14 | οἰκοδεσπότης 35 | ὀφθαλμός 13 | περιβάλλω 24 |
| μηκέτι 25 | οἰκοδομέω 19 | ὄφις 32 | περιπατέω 13 |
| μήν 28 | οἰκοδομή 28 | ὄχλος 10 | περισσεύω 19 |
| μήποτε 23 | οἰκονόμος 40 | ὀψία 32 | περισσός 25 |
| μήτε 21 | οἶκος 12 | | περισσοτέρως 37 |
| μήτηρ 14 | οἰκουμένη 31 | πάθημα 30 | περιστερά 40 |
| μήτι 28 | οἶνος 21 | παιδεύω 34 | περιτέμνω 29 |
| μικρός 17 | οἷος 32 | παιδίον 17 | περιτομή 20 |
| μιμνήσκομαι 25 | ὀλίγος 19 | παιδίσκη 34 | πετεινά 33 |
| μισέω 19 | ὅλος 12 | παῖς 24 | πέτρα 30 |
| μισθός 22 | ὀμνύω 23 | παλαιός 27 | πηγή 37 |
| μνῆμα 39 | ὁμοθυμαδόν 37 | πάλιν 11 | πιάζω 35 |
| μνημεῖον 19 | ὅμοιος 18 | παντοκράτωρ 40 | πίμπλημι 24 |
| μνημονεύω 26 | ὁμοιόω 31 | πάντοτι 19 | πίνω 14 |
| μοιχεύω 31 | ὁμοίως 21 | παρά 10 | πίπτω 14 |
| μόνος 17 | ὁμολογέω 24 | παραβολή 17 | πιστεύω 9 |
| μύρον 32 | ὀνειδίζω 37 | παραγγέλλω 21 | πίστις 9 |
| μυστήριον 22 | ὄνομα 9 | παραγίνομαι 19 | πιστός 15 |
| μωρός 32 | ὀνομάζω 40 | παράγω 37 | πλανάω 19 |
| | | παραδίδωμι 11 | πλάνη 40 |

πλατεῖα 40
πλείων 16
πλεονεξία 40
πληγή 25
πλῆθος 21
πληθύνω 35
πλήν 21
πλήρης 30
πληρόω 14
πλήρωμα 29
πλησίον 29
πλοῖον 15
πλούσιος 22
πλουτέω 35
πλοῦτος 25
πνεῦμα 10
πνευματικός 24
πόθεν 22
ποιέω 8
ποικίλος 40
ποιμαίνω 38
ποιμήν 28
ποῖος 21
πόλεμος 28
πόλις 11
πολλάκις 29
πολύς 10
πονηρός 14
πορεύομαι 11
πορνεία 24
πόρνη 35
πόρνος 40
πόσος 23
ποταμός 29
πότε 27
ποτέ 22
ποτήριον 21
ποτίζω 31
ποῦ 17
πούς 13
πρᾶγμα 38
πράσσω 19
πραΰτης 38
πρεσβύτερος 15
πρίν 34
πρό 17
προάγω 26
πρόβατον 19
προέρχομαι 40
πρόθεσις 36
προκαρτερέω 40
πρός 8

προσδέχομαι 33
προσδοκάω 30
προσέρχομαι 14
προσευχή 20
προσεύχομαι 14
προσέχω 24
προσκαλέομαι 22
προσκυνέω 16
προσλαμβάνω 36
προστίθημι 28
προσφέρω 17
πρόσωπον 14
πρότερος 38
προφητεία 27
προφητεύω 22
προφήτης 12
πρωΐ 36
πρῶτος 13
πτωχός 20
πύλη 40
πυλών 28
πυνθάνομαι 38
πῦρ 15
πωλέω 25
πῶλος 36
πῶς 12
πώς 34

ῥαββί 30
ῥάβδος 36
ῥῆμα 15
ῥίζα 30
ῥύομαι 29

σάββατον 15
σαλεύω 31
σάλπιγξ 38
σαλπίζω 36
σάρξ 12
σεαυτοῦ 18
σέβομαι 40
σεισμός 33
σημεῖον 15
σήμερον 18
σῖτος 33
σιωπάω 40
σκανδαλίζω 21
σκάνδαλον 31
σκεῦος 25
σκηνή 26
σκοτία 29
σκότος 21

σός 23
σοφία 17
σοφός 26
σπείρω 17
σπέρμα 18
σπλάγχνα 38
σπλαγχνίζομαι 36
σπουδάζω 38
σπουδή 36
σταυρός 23
σταυρόω 18
στέφανος 28
στήκω 36
στηρίζω 33
στόμα 15
στρατηγός 40
στρατιώτης 23
στρέφω 25
σύ 8
συγγενής 40
συζητέω 40
συκῆ 30
συλλαμβάνω 30
συμφέρω 31
σύν 12
συνάγω 15
συναγωγή 16
σύνδουλος 40
συνέδριον 25
συνείδησις 21
συνεργός 34
συνέρχομαι 21
συνέχω 36
συνίημι 23
συνίστημι 30
σφάζω 40
σφόδρα 38
σφραγίζω 31
σφραγίς 30
σχίζω 38
σῴζω 12
σῶμα 12
σωτήρ 24
σωτηρία 17

τάλαντον 33
ταπεινόω 33
ταράσσω 28
τάσσω 40
ταχέως 40
ταχύ 36
τε 11

τέκνον 13
τέλειος 27
τελειόω 25
τελευτάω 38
τελέω 22
τέλος 19
τελώνης 26
τέρας 30
τεσσαράκοντα 26
τέσσαρες 20
τέταρτος 40
τηρέω 15
τίθημι 13
τίκτω 28
τιμάω 26
τιμή 18
τίμιος 34
τις 8
τίς 8
τοιοῦτος 16
τολμάω 30
τόπος 13
τοσοῦτος 27
τότε 11
τράπεζα 31
τρεῖς 15
τρέχω 27
τριάκοντα 38
τρίς 36
τρίτος 17
τρόπος 34
τροφή 30
τυγχάνω 36
τύπος 31
τύπτω 34
τυφλός 17

ὑγιαίνω 36
ὑγιής 36
ὕδωρ 15
υἱός 10
ὑμέτερος 38
ὑπάγω 15
ὑπακοή 31
ὑπακούω 26
ὑπαντάω 38
ὑπάρχω 16
ὑπέρ 11
ὑπηρέτης 26
ὑπό 10
ὑπόδημα 40
ὑποκάτω 38

ὥσπερ ξένοι χαίρουσι πατρίδα βλέπειν,
οὕτως καὶ τοῖς κάμνουσι βιβλίου τέλος.